KICK START YOUR OWN MARTIAL ARTS SCHOOL

HOW TO SET-UP AND RUN A SUCCESSFUL MARTIAL ARTS BUSINESS

TALIB FEHLHABER

FOREWORD BY GEOFF THOMPSON

bookshaker

First published in the United Kingdom 2012
by Bookshaker.com

"A camel is stronger than a man; an elephant is larger; a lion has greater valour; cattle can eat more than man; birds are more virile. Man was made for the purpose of learning."

Al-Ghazali

This book is dedicated to my lovely parents on whose shoulders I stand today. Special mention goes to the loving memory of my late father Jürgen Fehlhaber, who never got to witness my successes.

PRAISE

"This book will give you the "Need To Know Info" on starting but more importantly running your Martial Art School. I've been in the coaching game quite a few years now and I was getting all enthusiastic and revved up whilst reading this book. It's given my coaching a new lease of life."
Jason Owers – Head Coach of Combat Camp, Gravesend, Kent, UK

"This book is very comprehensive and I really like the conversational style of writing. It is compelling and I found it hard to put down."
Alex Buxton – 3rd Dan Wado Ryu Karate Instructor, Luton Higash Karate

"Not only do I highly recommend this book, I also think that it is the best book on the market for anyone seriously considering martial arts teaching as a career... I wish I'd had this valuable information at the beginning of my own teaching career."
Geoff Thompson, Autor of "Watch My Back", 7th Dan Shotokan Karate

ACKNOWLEDGEMENTS

Ultimately all praise and gratitude belongs to the single creative force in the universe, which goes by many names.

If someone would have told me ten years ago that I would end up running my own thriving, full-time martial arts school in the city centre of Norwich, I would have probably just laughed at them. If that same person predicted that I also would become a published author, writing a book on that very subject matter, I would have strongly advised them to increase the dosage of whatever they seemed to be on.

But here we are! The book is out, with its own website, and my school is still running despite one of the toughest economic recessions in living memory. It seems I must be doing something right.

However, no man is an island and all this could not have been achieved without the help and support of some very special people in my life. So credit must be given where it is due. Firstly, I must express my undying love and gratitude to my soul mate, best friend and devoted wife Salama, who for the last twenty years has not only endured my ramblings but aided and supported me all the way. I often wonder where I would be without you my love and I am looking forward to what the next twenty years will bring us.

The chief "blame" for me even to consider writing a book lies with my friend and fellow martial artist, Mr. Nial Adams of PUSH Marketing, who, starting back in 2011 advised, coached and supported me to take on such a challenge. Nial was also instrumental in designing and providing the website for this book.

I would also like to acknowledge all my students, past and present, as well as all the instructors and teachers who have allowed me to learn and absorb so very much over the years. I would particularly like to express my appreciation and gratitude to my teacher, Sifu Nick Smart of Chorley, Lancs., who really instilled me with the passion and love for the art of Wing Chun Kung Fu and who got me started as a junior instructor back in 1993.

Last but not least I would like to thank my publisher and fellow martial artist, Joe Gregory, who has provided me with a lot of great support and feedback in getting my very first book out there.

A big thank you to you all! I look forward to the next project.

FOREWORD

Kick Start Your Own Martial Arts School is a fabulous, invaluable, inspiring, informative, well written and refreshingly honest book on running a successful, full time martial arts club without compromising on standard and integrity.

Not only do I highly recommend this book, I also think that it is the best book on the market for anyone seriously considering martial arts teaching as a career.

This book is comprehensive and easy to follow. Its author, Talib Fehlhaber, has left out nothing in his quest to give the reader – the aspiring MA entrepreneur – everything he needs, not only to set up a tenable business, but also to maintain and grow it.

I wish I'd had this valuable information at the beginning of my own teaching career.

It is not enough simply to open a school and expect students to fall through the door just because you are there. As the author says, it is common in the martial arts to be a black belt in class, and a white belt in business. This does not make for a winning formula.

There is so much in this book, so many useful tips, ideas and inspirations, that I would fail in my duty if I tried to list them all here. All I will say is, *please take my recommendation and buy this book, you will not be disappointed.* If you implement Talib's suggestions it literally could mean the difference between failure and massive success.

Highly recommended.

Geoff Thompson
Bafta winning writer, teacher and martial artist
www.geoffthompson.com

CONTENTS

INTRODUCTION

The dream of one day running your own martial arts school or club is something many martial arts instructors nurture. If you are anything like me however, you probably have never been told by your instructor how to set one up from scratch or how to run a school successfully with dozens of happy and paying students. The reasons for that could be manifold. Perhaps your instructor(s) didn't really know how to do that either and just kind of stumbled into it themselves or because they just didn't want to educate their next competition. One thing is clear; to set-up and to run a thriving martial arts school takes a lot more than just a black belt and some guts. In fact it has nothing to do with how good you are at your chosen style or even if you are good instructor.

This book is written for the ambitious martial artist who might perhaps already be teaching and wants to take his/her class or club to the next level. Perhaps you are a complete newcomer to teaching or you are assisting an instructor in a class and are merely tinkering with the idea of starting your own club. In any case this book is for you. It is also ideal if you are perhaps thinking of returning to class teaching after some time off. Beyond that it can also serve as a teaching manual if you are planning to run an instructors course.

Whatever your current level of expertise, you will gain some valuable insights and guidance on all aspects of starting and running a profitable martial arts school – either part-time or on a full-time basis. The book will give you the benefit of many years of hard earned expertise from someone who has actually been there and done it for himself with minimum help, no previous experience, and zero start-up capital. This book will shave years off your own learning curve and will save you untold amounts of time, money and hassle.

I make no apologies for any future changes, as this book merely represents my current understanding and experiences. Things such as changes in the economy, new trends in the world of martial arts, as well as any new insights, will inevitably help me to evolve and refine my views.

HOW IS THIS BOOK DIFFERENT FROM OTHER BOOKS ON THE SUBJECT?

All of the (few) books which are currently available on starting and/or running your own martial arts school are predominantly focused on the U.S. market and although they contain valuable information they require quite a bit of re-thinking to make many of those suggestions and assumptions work over here in Europe land. For example, it is not uncommon to find martial arts schools in the U.S. in strip malls next to a Wallmart or a Starbucks, some with up to a thousand students! In all the years that I have been involved in the martial arts in various countries across Europe, I have never even once seen a martial arts school in a shopping centre anywhere. In fact if anything they tend to be tucked away quite nicely in church halls and community centres. Plus many American Dojos seem to be a lot more focused on commerce, especially if they are run as a business and not as an extension of the instructor's ego.

Throughout this book I'm trying not to use too much business jargon as it doesn't help to make things clearer, particularly to the uninitiated, so if you have an MBA "Good for you!" but you don't need one in order to read, understand and implement the tried and tested material in this book.

Michael Lebouef, a business consultant and author, once wrote; "A great deal of what we read in medical, technical and academic documents is little more than the old professional snow job game – If you can't dazzle them with brilliance, baffle them with B.S. The

2

purpose of a great deal of the jargon is to ensure the future of the experts rather than the consumer."

Before we get into the nitty gritty of setting up our own school I would first like to give you an overview of what's to come by listing some of the typical rookie mistakes, many of which are practised more diligently than Katas in the world of martial arts.

WHY AM I SHARING MY "SECRETS" WITH POTENTIAL COMPETITORS?

When I began work on this book, people said, "Talib, you must be crazy! You've had to learn all this stuff the hard way and now you're sharing everything for the price of a single martial arts class! Aren't you scared your competitors will get this stuff?"

I must admit, I did have my reservations but, as you'll discover when you've read the whole of this book, there is a method to my apparent madness.

For now though, let me share a few of my motivations for imparting my hard-won knowledge with you:

I'M PASSIONATE ABOUT RAISING STANDARDS FOR MARTIAL ARTS SCHOOLS IN THE UK AND EUROPE

There are currently far too many poorly run, uninsured and frankly dangerous outfits operating in the world today and if this book prevents one would-be martial arts entrepreneur from taking the wrong path I'll be happier. Also, if my competitors do read this book and raise their standards as a result, then we all win by the improved image of martial arts schools. In essence, just as good competition helps us raise our martial arts game so it goes with business.

I WANT TO COUNTER THE (FRANKLY) AWFUL ADVICE FROM GET-RICH-QUICK BUSINESS 'GURUS'

The McDojo phenomenon of cookie-cutter martial arts schools that prevails in the USA doesn't always translate well when it's taken wholesale into the UK. In fact, the focus is often single-mindedly on profit over providing value which leads to poor teaching standards and a bad deal for students. Don't get me wrong, I'm certainly all for people systemizing what works and repeating it – so if you see yourself with a global chain of martial arts centres this book will help – but there's a right way and a wrong way to do it.

I'M WRITING THE BOOK I WISH I'D HAD WHEN I STARTED OUT

When I first started teaching back in 1993 and then set-up my full-time school in 2004, I had to learn the hard way about a lot of what works. This book will help to shave years off your learning curve and ensure you succeed more quickly. Plus, this business has been good to me so this book is one small way to give something back to those who follow.

I WANT TO LEAVE A LASTING LEGACY AND PROVE THE DOUBTERS WRONG

I'll admit this one is motivated by ego. When I decided to pursue a career as a martial arts teacher many people, often with good intentions, tried to talk me out of it. They urged me to get a "proper job" instead. This book will serve as a lasting reminder for many years to come that not only is martial arts instruction a viable "proper career" but that the doubters were wrong!

WE ALL NEED TO TAKE THINGS EASIER AT SOME POINT

I've been treading the mats for over three decades now and my feet are getting sore! I'm gradually delegating the day-to-day running of my martial arts school to my assistant instructors so I can spend more time as a mentor and business advisor, talking business with people like you. Sitting in a cosy office or driving a car will give my feet a break and writing this guide will ensure I can refer my successors to a reliable and consistent operations manual. At the end of this book you'll find details of a unique free mini-course and my contact details, so if you want more hands-on support to improve or start your martial arts business, get in touch.

WHO IS THIS BOOK FOR?

If you can answer yes to one or more of the following statements then this book has been written for you. The world needs more martial arts schools like the one you can build.

- You're looking to turn your passion for martial arts into a viable, full-time income and career.
- You're prepared and willing to set-up an ethical, professional martial arts business that genuinely improves the health, skills and lives of your students.
- You understand that there is much more to setting up and succeeding than simply being good at martial arts.
- You love martial arts and genuinely want to share what you know with eager students in return for a fair reward for the value you share.

WHO IS THIS BOOK NOT FOR?

If any of the following statements describe your motivation for starting your own martial arts school then I'd strongly urge you to reconsider. However, as you hold in your hand a manual for doing things the right way, I suggest you read on. You might change your mind.

- You're in it solely for the money and think the rising popularity of martial arts as a way to fitness could be an easy ticket to riches.
- You're in it because you want an adoring following of students who think you're the toughest guy on the planet.
- You've watched a ton of martial arts instructional DVDs and movies and think there's a space for your own take on martial arts called "Joe-Fu" (replace 'Joe' with your own name).

HOW TO GET THE MOST FROM THIS BOOK

If you're just at the planning stage of your new business with nothing in place then I suggest you read this book from start to finish. It's a comprehensive guide to everything you'll need to know and do to set-up your own martial arts school and succeed. As your business grows you can refer to specific chapters as a refresher and reminder of what you're supposed to be doing.

If you're already running a martial arts school or club and would like to make it more efficient or run it more like a business and have a specific challenge, perhaps to attract new students, then I suggest you review the detailed table of contents and go directly to the chapter that best reflects your needs.

Right, we're almost ready to begin, but first I want you to be aware of...

THE TOP TEN MARTIAL ARTS SCHOOL OWNER ROOKIE MISTAKES

1. YOU HAVE TO BE A BLACK BELT/MASTER LEVEL TO TEACH

Perhaps the most common rookie mistake. Although you need to know what you are teaching you don't need to be a grand master to teach beginners. Much of this stems from a low self-esteem on the side of the instructor and is simply a self limiting fantasy.

2. THINKING THAT YOUR STUDENTS ARE JUST LIKE YOU

We all tend to see the world from the inside out, i.e. as seasoned experts with years or even decades of experience. This can lead to some expensive assumptions if we think that students are just like us and that they like or choose things just like us.

3. IF I BUILD IT THEY WILL COME

Only relying on word of mouth propaganda or thinking that it is OK to wait for new students just because you have a great looking Dojo is risky. People will not queue around the block to join your school just because of a fancy website.

4. BEING FLATTERED BY TURNOVER

It is not difficult to make money by teaching martial arts, but it is quite another thing to be profitable and to make a decent living out of it for many years consistently. Most school owners massively lack financial education, which is costing them £1,000s every year.

5. NOT CHARGING ENOUGH

Most martial arts instructors are over qualified and under paid. There often seems to be a conflict of interests when it comes to charging for classes. Running a thriving and profitable martial arts school means understanding when, how and how much to charge.

6. AVOIDING THE DIFFICULT TASKS

Dealing with what is familiar and comfortable is normal, but it doesn't help to tackle the boring or daunting tasks, which are often the more important ones. Creating avoidance is one sure fire way to turn your school into a lead Zeppelin.

7. NOT HAVING A PLAN

People spend more time planning their annual holidays than on any other aspect of their life. Underestimating the importance of – even a basic – business or marketing plan can have dire consequences. You have heard the adage "Failing to plan is planning to fail".

8. LISTENING TO YOUR MUM

We all like to hear when somebody sings our praises and compliments us on our many achievements and there is nothing wrong with that. Listening to anyone who doesn't agree with you on the other hand is a whole different kind of skill.

9. FAILING TO DELEGATE

No-one will share your degree of passion and enthusiasm for your school. This is one of your greatest strengths and at the same time is going to be your biggest problem when trying to grow your school. You have to learn to work on your business rather than in it. Sounds crazy?

10. NOT DOING IT AT ALL

I left the worst mistake for last. Many fledging martial arts professionals allow themselves to be held back and even stopped by rumours, myths and worries. It can ultimately lead to you not getting started at all.

PART ONE

PLANNING AND PREPARATION

KNOW YOURSELF:
MENTAL PREPARATION

"All glory comes from daring to begin."
EUGENE F. WARE

Before getting into the more practical aspects of setting up and running a successful martial arts school, I would like to address an area that has become vital to me (and to my trainee instructors, later).

You are in for an amazing ride and a huge learning experience that will push you right against and often way beyond your comfort zone. Being your own boss and having to deal with the pressures and responsibilities that come with that can be challenging and sometimes even daunting. Running your own show requires a good amount of mental toughness and staying power, especially when things don't go as you expect them to. This is of course no reason not to take the plunge, but forewarned is being forearmed.

SUCCESS IS NOT A MATTER OF LUCK

"Success is a matter of luck. If you want proof, ask any failure."
EARL WILSON

When you talk to the average man or women on the street about successful people, most will probably tell you that they somehow got lucky because they had superior intelligence, better education, or were somehow born with a silver spoon in their mouth.

Why some people are more successful than others has fascinated psychologists and researchers for decades and has subsequently spawned many studies and books that have been published on what is now called the *Success Psychology*. The one thing all of these investigations have found is that the majority of successful people have in fact started out with some kind of disadvantage, i.e. little or no education, poor upbringings, average intelligence and some even with disabilities.

Beethoven was deaf, Milton was blind, Einstein couldn't talk until he was four and did not read until he was seven. Before writing her famous novels, J.K. Rowling was nearly penniless, severely depressed, divorced and trying to raise a child on her own while being on state benefits.

And I can't say that I was exactly lucky either. I come from a broken home with an abusive father, which caused me to spend five years of my youth in a foster home, where I had to (quite literally) fight to survive. I dropped out of three different job training positions without completing any one of them and barely made it out of a religious cult, which held me mentally captive for four years and made me question my entire *raison d'être*.

Yet here I am today; an internationally recognised martial arts master, published author, mentor, seminar leader and public speaker. I speak four languages, three of them fluently. I have travelled to over twenty countries around the word, and lived in four. And I have been running my own successful business for over eight years without any training, support or start-up capital.

So, what makes some people succeed while others struggle to get by? I believe that it has absolutely nothing to do with intelligence, education, wealth or even hard work. But it has everything to do with the way we perceive and think about ourselves. Many people foolishly believe that their own limitations are the yardstick by which they should measure success. They cannot think in terms of wealth or abundance because their thought habits have been steeped in poverty, misery and failure. And they reject different ways of thinking simply because they are not the same as their own.

The one thing that drives people into success is the single minded desire to succeed. If this burning desire is backed up by self-belief, or faith, it becomes rocket fuel for the soul.

This reminds me of a story I heard many years ago about an immigrant who came to these shores from some war-torn part of Africa; alone and completely penniless. He was put through the regular immigration channels and brought up to speed on how things work over here. At one point however he misunderstood his interpreter who, to his mind at least, told him that if he applied himself he will become a millionaire. Not that he CAN become one, but that he WILL become one.

Armed with this certainty and the vivid memory of his war ravaged home country he started to throw himself at this golden opportunity and did not rest until he had achieved his first million. In his mind he could not fail as he simply believed what he was told. This "false" belief coupled with the burning desire to escape poverty and attain riches made him a wealthy and respected man. He didn't simply hope or wish to be wealthy, or perhaps thought it might be pretty nifty. He totally and whole-heartedly committed himself to his goal, as failure was not an option.

The same can be true for you and your ambitions in running a thriving martial arts school. It is not a question of luck or winning the lottery. Think back to what it took for you to reach your black belt or instructor level in your chosen style. It didn't just land in your lap, you didn't quit until you finally held it in your hands. If you have what it takes to earn a black belt you definitely pre-qualify as a business success.

You will succeed provided you have definite purpose and do not doubt that success will be yours. The strange thing is that you will find it easy and not hard to do. Why? Because hundreds of people with much less going for themselves have done so before you and because I am telling you how to do it, step by step. All you have to do is not quit.

THE IMPOSTER SYNDROME

A very common phenomenon when you are starting to become more successful and suddenly find yourself with a hundred or so students is a creeping feeling that this is somehow too good to be true or that somebody is going to call your bluff any day now.

The Oscar winning Hollywood actor Paul Newman once mentioned in an interview that he always feared that one day someone would push through the crowd, grab him by the arm and say. "It's over Newman. It was all a mistake. You're coming back to painting houses." What he was describing is what Psychologists call the *Impostor Syndrome*. I certainly can relate to that, as I have often stopped and asked myself if this is really happening? Can this really be happening to a guy like me? Is this all too good to be true? The thing to remember here is that you are in fact good enough and that you do deserve the success and kudos.

It all stems from a healthy and positive self-image, which is something that needs constant care.

BULLET-PROOF SELF-BELIEF

"It's lack of faith that makes people afraid of meeting challenges, and I believe in myself."
MUHAMMAD ALI

Of all the skills you must build as a successful martial arts professional, bullet-proof self-belief should be on the top of your list.

When we observe political, military or economic leaders it becomes immediately obvious that the majority of them share a very healthy (even if distorted) image of themselves and are respected and admired for it. You might even be forgiven for thinking that some of these people are charismatic.

Hence the way you perceive yourself ultimately determines how you are perceived by others. And because we do not sell anything tangible in our classes you are therefore "the product". As a martial arts instructor it is vital that your positive self-image is intact, without being loud or overbearing of course. Furthermore you need to understand that you can only act in a way that is consistent with the way you perceive yourself if you don't want to be a fake or live a lie. Besides, people will sooner or later pick up on a false or assumed image, as it is impossible to be consistent with something that you are not.

As world-renowned business author and speaker Brian Tracy said:

> *"The person we believe ourselves to be will always*
> *act in a manner consistent with our self-image."*

This consistency is absolutely crucial to the way you reward and/or punish yourself for things and, perhaps more importantly, how you are perceived by others as a role model. But don't worry, you don't have to be Mr. or Ms. Perfect to make it as a valued and successful instructor and/or school owner. As long as you are true to yourself, people will either get you or they won't. Either way is just fine. There is really no need to try to be everything to everybody. In fact it's the worst thing you can do and we will talk about this later.

Although physical appearances can be important, they can also be quite deceptive. Many a competent and experienced instructor and/or master I have come across are overweight, balding, or cross eyed and some even have disabilities. I have been suffering from a non-contagious skin problem called Psoriasis for years and although it's more cosmetic in nature it has never stopped me or put my students off.

The point I am trying to make here is that something is only an issue if you make it so. What good are you ultimately going to be to your students if all you have to offer is the fact that you could feature on a *Men's Health* front cover? Of course health, fitness and wellbeing are important, but they very much start on the inside with your thoughts about who you are and to what you aspire. This positive self-image, as any motivational speaker can tell you, is directly linked to your attitude towards life and ultimately how successful you are, regardless of how you define success. This positive self-image is also going to be important as it determines how well you are able to respond to the challenges and pressures that life in general and a buzzing martial arts school in particular, can throw at you. It is all about how you see yourself and what tune you are playing in your head.

SELF TALK

"One day I sat thinking, almost in despair; a hand fell on my shoulder and a voice said reassuringly: cheer up, things could get worse. So I cheered up and, sure enough, things got worse."
JAMES HAGERTY

We like to think that only people with "issues" talk to themselves, but the fact is that everybody is constantly talking to themselves, albeit some more audibly that others.

Self-talk is in fact extremely important when it comes to personal performance as any top athlete or soldier will tell you. Many people have survived ridiculous odds and ordeals, while others failed or died simply because they gave up hope.

You are equipped with the most powerful weapon ever conceived – your mind. It is such a powerful tool and can quite literally create alternate realities, all due to the things you keep telling yourself. As the industrialist Henry Ford is quoted to have said:

*"If you think you can do a thing or think
you can't do a thing, you're right."*

Studies on patients with multiple personality disorders have shown that as the patient adopts an alternate personality everything about that person changes, their body language, their accent and even in some rare cases the colour of their eyes!

You should be aware of your self-talk, i.e. the way you communicate with yourself. It is a conscious and ongoing process. It is this ability to choose how you respond to various challenges, which is one of the hall-marks of highly successful people. It is particularly important when things might not start or go as well as you are expecting or when people let you down. This is, in my experience, quite often the case as you set your standards way above those of others and because you simply expect more from life. There is really nothing wrong with that.

Over the years of being self-employed I have learned that being the boss can be a lonely but rewarding existence. You have to make decisions that can bring you handsome returns on the one hand or debts and disappointment on the other. That is life for the entrepreneur, either get used to it or get back to 9 to 5 where your decisions are made for you. There will be times where you wish somebody would just tell you what to do or when to do it, which is only normal – especially if it reflects the pattern of your previous working life.

But where to start? How can you begin to change and improve the image that you hold of yourself, particularly if it is not helping and supporting you? Well, you have to start liking yourself to begin with; you have to be the one who is telling yourself that you are a great person; you have to tell yourself that you like yourself and you have to do it consciously every day.

> *"It took me a long time not to judge myself*
> *through someone else's eyes."*
> **SALLY FIELD**

I really cannot over emphasise the importance of keeping yourself mentally fit and healthy, because, just as it is in a fight or a tournament, running your own martial arts business is mind over matter every time.

There have been plenty of studies on the effects and workings of the mind and since man has understood how easy it is to manipulate the way people think, it has been shamelessly exploited by advertisers and politicians.

In his book *The Power of Your Subconscious Mind*, Joseph Murphy uses the analogy of a captain and his ship to illustrate the different roles of the conscious and unconscious mind. The captain represents the conscious mind, who is charge of the ship, which represents the unconscious mind. The captain operates and controls all the instruments of the ship and thereby the ships direction. Below deck, are the engine room and the crew who are really the power house of the ship. The crew does what the captain commands and doesn't argue back. So if the captain should decide to run the ship onto the rocks the crew would simply follow the order and go full steam ahead to their doom. The subconscious works in much the same way. It takes whatever information it is supplied with and makes it a reality.

Thinking patterns or habits cannot be simply removed; they have to be replaced by other patterns or habits. All this has been understood and practised for millennia in all belief systems and religions. These practices are called mantras or prayers or reminders. If you are practicing a religion or spiritual path, try focusing your prayers and meditations on how you feel about yourself and actively replace any self-doubt, criticism or blame with the simple message that you like yourself. Just repeat that to yourself every day at least a hundred times. I promise you that even after only a short period of doing so, you will notice a positive change in the way you perceive yourself which is crucial for the way others see you. Think about it, who wants to be around a self-loathing pessimist?

This brings us elegantly to our next point; other people.

YOU ARE AS GOOD AS THE PEOPLE AROUND YOU

Apart from believing that you are the real deal (the fact that you are reading and agreeing with this is testimony to that) you need to also create an environment that allows you to flourish. It is hard enough to face some of the challenges that being self-reliant can bring. You really don't need to have to compensate for other peoples negativity on top of that. I know this may sound quite arrogant and ruthless, but please believe me when I tell you that you need to cut out *any* negative chatter, which is inspired by fear, jealousy or just plain ignorance. I've eliminated much of my TV consumption on that basis, especially what is passed off as "news" these days, is almost exclusively just bad news and hype. Inevitably people around you will feel threatened and inferior as you aspire to lead and aim for bigger and better things, but that is a reflection of their insecurities, with which they ultimately need to deal. If anybody takes issue with whom you want to become then do yourself a favour and walk away from them. And if you can't do that because these are your parents or your partner then don't discuss your plans or success stories with them. Prove them wrong one day by driving your spanking new Ferrari up their drive-way or buy them a house to shut them up.

The following quote has always been a source of inspiration for me.

"Our deepest fear is not that we are inadequate. Our deepest fear is that we are powerful beyond measure. It is our light, not our darkness, that most frightens us. We ask ourselves, who am I to be brilliant, successful, talented and fabulous? Actually, who are you NOT to be? You are a child of God. Your playing small doesn't serve the world. There's nothing enlightened about shrinking so that other people won't feel insecure around you. We are born to make manifest the glory that is within us. It's not just in some of us; it's in EVERYONE! And as we let our light shine, we unconsciously give other people permission to do the same. As we are liberated from our own fear, our presence automatically liberates others."

NELSON MANDELA, QUOTING MARIANNE WILLIAMSON,

IN HIS INAUGURAL SPEECH, 1994

YOUR MUM IS A "LIAR" – OR WHY YOU SHOULDN'T LISTEN TO PEOPLE WHO SING YOUR PRAISES

In the process of creating that ever-important nourishing environment, you might need to change your peer group. Even if the people that surround you don't necessarily try to bring you back down to their comfort level Already successful individuals tend to have a very powerful impact on others by reminding them that success is not only achievable but almost inevitable given the right ingredients and nurturing surroundings. It's just like in martial arts training when you have the opportunity to train with other black belts and masters, it not only improves what you are doing it also inspires you to become more like them. This is done simply because they will challenge you and your current level of understanding. Imagine if you could be around these kinds of people regularly, how long would it take you to also become a master or even a grandmaster? But apart from inspiring you they also can help to bring you down to earth and keep you on track. I count myself very privileged to be able to get a few hours with people who are very successful and have been through some of the fears, struggles and challenges that await you. The one thing that I value the most is that they tell you straight if you are barking up the wrong tree. There have been many meetings where I thought that this next idea is going to impress them, only to come out of the meeting with a completely different vantage point. For that reason you should be careful when talking to your nearest and dearest about your plans and ambitions as they often just like to tell you what you want to hear. Not because they like to misguide you, but because they probably are out of their depths and don't want to see you get disheartened by their criticisms. Fellow business people however can, and should, be brutally direct and honest as there is often a lot at stake; complementing you on your obvious successes doesn't really help to keep you alert to the next challenges.

As important as these role models are as benchmarks for success, you might not be able to have multi-millionaires as your day-to-day buddies, but it is easier than you might think to regularly meet and befriend (much) more successful people. Ten years ago just meeting a millionaire or a school owner with a thousand students would have been pretty cool for me. Without trying to sound too blasé, enjoying the company of successful people today is something that just naturally happens.

Being around successful people will change your attitude towards what is achievable, and more importantly, towards money.

ARE YOU A MARTIAL ART SELL-OUT TOO?

The world of martial arts is a very unique scene with every kind of strange and wonderful person. There are as many different motivations for practicing martial arts as there are people who practice them.

Due to the fact that many martial arts styles are of a far eastern origin and are influenced by philosophies and religions like Buddhism and Taoism, many practitioners and instructors treat their particular style a bit like a religion or at least some kind of pseudo-religion. This has the perhaps predictable side effect that many instructors feel somewhat uneasy with charging for their expertise and time, even if they themselves have spent many years and literally thousands of Dollars, Pounds or Euros of their hard-earned money to acquire their skills and insights. Not to mention all the travelling, uncomfortable nights in hotels, B&B's and on gym floors.

It always strikes me as odd that these colleagues suddenly seem to suffer from selective amnesia when it's their turn to teach and charge for the privilege. Don't get me wrong; I respect the fact that for many martial arts enthusiasts their training is never more than a passion and they have managed to find themselves in it. But this doesn't therefore mean that charging for quality tuition is equal to getting rich at the expense of your students and therefore selling out, or pimping, the arts. If you are inclined to think that way you have to seriously drop that attitude if you want to start and run a profitable school.

If you were to compare this to any other sport or human endeavour, the absurdity of such an attitude becomes immediately apparent.

Would you accuse a former professional football player or a concert guitarist of pimping his art simply because he/she charges (even exuberant amounts) for his/her expertise? Is that person a sell out because they are making money from sharing their knowledge and hard won insights? Of course not! These people are frequently referred to as being highly successful – some even with celebrity status – and are seen by others as role models. Otherwise all consultants and experts would be nothing but expensive prostitutes!

KNOW YOURSELF: MENTAL PREPARATION

So why should the martial arts be any different? I think it's easy to see that it is often selfish motives and pure envy that keep unsuccessful people bickering in online forums and magazines.

MONEY FOR NOTHING AND KICKS FOR FREE

To put it simply, money is just not as big a deal as you think. The only time when money feels like a big deal is when you don't have it. This unfortunately is when emotions such as jealousy, envy, bitterness and anger can surface, when you see that others have money or don't seem to deserve their success. These feelings are only natural; we all have had them at some point in our lives, but what is important is that we don't allow them to control us.

As information marketer Peter Thompson so rightly said, "Money is the silent applause for a job well done."

I always like to use a carpentry analogy when I explain this to my trainee instructors. If you are cutting a board with a saw you will generate sawdust; it's an inevitable by-product. However, very few people cut boards to get saw dust. In the same way that money is very much a result of correct thinking, it's a by-product and will appear if you do the right things that need to be done consistently, which will generate a steady flow of income.

Business author Brian Tracy refers to thinking as the highest paid activity for any successful entrepreneur. As he says: "Quality thinking gets you quality results."

The reason I say this is because many people, especially in our industry, get this the wrong way around and start doing business to chase a quick buck or maybe because their money management skills are so poor, perhaps spending more than they earn, which forces them to look for short-term profits. If your students can see the value in what you are offering, not only will they stay with you longer they will be more than happy to pay you for it.

In conclusion, you need to develop a different perspective if money presents a challenge or distraction for you. A simple decision to look at money more as "saw dust" rather than the "be all and end all" will go some way to help you to change the way that you may be influenced by money. Resist the temptation to let somebody else handle all your money matters or you will never learn.

Differentiate between those people who are trying to help you to achieve you goals and those who stand in the way of that success and try to hold you back. Success is not so much about what you know, but who you know and to whom you allow yourself to listen.

> *"Don't go where the path may lead, go where*
> *there is no path and leave a trail."*
> **RALPH WALDO EMERSON**

Most people will not venture outside their comfort zone as they are afraid they will fail. This is also one reason, in my humble opinion, why wealth tends to be distributed so unevenly as only a minority are willing to stick their necks out, because they know that there are big rewards to be had for venturing outside their comfort zones.

When I first picked up the keys to my very first full-time school in December 2004, I was still holding down a job as a mortgage adviser at a firm in Norwich. As you can imagine I was very excited about the fact that I had suddenly begun to realise my dream of a full-time school. Once I had returned to my desk in early January and still high on paint fumes and DIY, I found it increasingly difficult to concentrate on my job anymore. All my thoughts were with my new baby. So I had a decision to make; should I just hand in my notice and jump in at the deep end or should I play it safe and build up the school gradually in my spare time? I asked myself what the worst case scenario would be if I took the plunge. Why? Well, the worst case scenario for me was that I would probably have to find myself another job if I failed in making it as a full-time martial arts professional It was then that I realised that I was already in my worst case scenario of making some other guy rich. Without further ado I printed my notice on company stationery and handed it in and was off like a kid in a toy store.

Did I get everything right from the start? No, of course not I made some horrendous decisions over the years, but I learned from them (well, most of them). Eight years on I am still here to tell the story. This book should give you many of the important tools and insights that will help you to make a success of yourself without selling-out or compromising your integrity. The important thing is to believe in yourself, prepare as well as you can and above all to be consistent. The dream of one day owning your own thriving martial arts school is closer than you might think.

> *"Whatever the mind of a man can*
> *conceive and believe, it can achieve."*
> **NAPOLEON HILL**

RAPID RECAP – KNOW YOURSELF

- Don't get caught out by *Impostor Syndrome*.
- Develop and nurture rock solid self-belief.
- Don't believe your own hype (or compliments from your mum).
- Don't underestimate yourself or constantly judge yourself by other people's standards – you're as good, if not better, than the rest.
- Remember, it's not all about the money – there's much more to it than that.
- You're not selling-out by charging to pass on the knowledge you've acquired through long practice and financial investment.

SELF QUIZ: ARE YOU CUT OUT TO START AND RUN A MARTIAL ARTS SCHOOL?

Answer each question honestly: "yes" is worth 2 points, "no" is worth 0 points and "maybe" is worth 1 point.

1. Are you prepared to take the responsibility (blame) for everything when starting and/or running your own school, even if it isn't your fault?
   Yes ☐ No ☐ Maybe ☐

2. Are you prepared to work long hours, weekends, bank holidays and to come home at unsocial hours?
   Yes ☐ No ☐ Maybe ☐

3. Can you work under your own steam with no supervision or encouragement from others?
   Yes ☐ No ☐ Maybe ☐

4. Are you ready to take on the prospect of additional stress and potential failure?
   Yes ☐ No ☐ Maybe ☐

5. Have you got the backing of your loved ones?
   Yes ☐ No ☐ Maybe ☐

6. Are you prepared to constantly learn new stuff, become a reader and even travel for new information and insights?
   Yes ☐ No ☐ Maybe ☐

7. Will you be able to get by with little or no income for the first 12 month of your new venture?
   Yes ☐ No ☐ Maybe ☐

KNOW YOURSELF: MENTAL PREPARATION

8. Have you made proper plans to help you stay on course?
Yes ☐ No ☐ Maybe ☐

9. Are you prepared to quit your day time job (eventually)?
Yes ☐ No ☐ Maybe ☐

10. Do have a lifetime's worth of passion to teach martial arts and inspire others?
Yes ☐ No ☐ Maybe ☐

Total Scores

0 – 8 Points
I would have serious reservations in recommending that you take the plunge at this stage. It could be that you might have some misplaced romantic notions about running a martial arts school.
Go back to the drawing board and re-examine your reasons and motivations for making it as an independent school owner. Being realistic might save you and others a lot of time, money and un-wanted hassle.

9 – 15 Points
It looks like you have acquainted yourself with the realities of what life could throw at you during the set-up and starting phase of running a small one-man-band business. There is obviously still plenty of room for improvement, but given the right advice and support there seems to be a good chance you could actually make a success of it.

16 – 20 Points
You are definitely keen and ready to grab the bull by the horns, knowing full well that there are a lot of surprises waiting for you.

Failure and hard work don't seem to scare you. However make sure you don't fall victim to your own over enthusiasm and burn out early. There are no substitutes for a clear vision, proper planning and consistency.

KNOW YOUR BUSINESS

"There are three things to remember when teaching: know your stuff; know whom you are stuffing; and then stuff them elegantly."

LOLA MAY

WHAT BUSINESS YOU'RE REALLY IN

Being involved in the martial arts is one of the best, most versatile and most rewarding activities, of which you could hope to be a part, especially if you teach and inspire others. There is so much room for self-exploration and personal growth that I would find it difficult to come up with an area of human endeavour that would even come close. In my view, teaching and studying martial arts caters to every aspect of human needs and I'd like to prove it to you.

In 1943 the American psychologist Abraham Maslow submitted a paper on "A Theory of Human Motivation". In it he proposed a hierarchy of human needs to which everybody is subject, ranging from basic human needs like breathing, sleeping, eating and sex to higher needs of self-actualisation like creativity and morality. His theories have later become accepted as one of the mainstream ideas of psychology and human development. Teaching martial arts addresses every aspect of Maslow's hierarchy of needs.

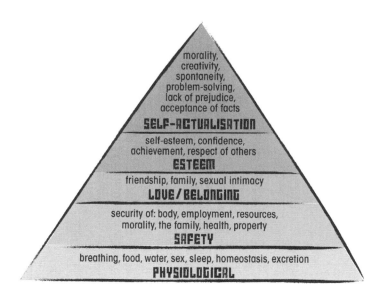

Physiological:

At the most basic level, learning martial arts enables you to educate your body through vigorous exercise and can help students to overcome sleeping disorders as well as helping to control their breathing as their physical condition improves. Physical fitness also helps to improve one's digestion and sex life.

Safety:

Most martial arts will give you the ability and confidence to defend yourself or at least have the confidence to walk away from a fight. Being able to defend yourself will also make you feel safer and more confident and you are able to better withstand stressful situations.

Love/Belonging:

Many people start their journey into the fighting arts because they want to make new friends and it is not uncommon for people to take their training friendships a step further – some even get married having got to know and trust each other in their classes. Many families find common purpose in training together in a style of their choosing.

Esteem:

Once certain levels of proficiency are achieved, many martial artists can enjoy the kudos and the achievement of the next belt or of being a black belt or an instructor. This would make them a role model for other students as well as for friends, family and co-workers. Black Belt is synonymous with excellence, skill and achievement.

Self Actualisation:

At the highest level of martial arts lies self actualisation and the attainment of a higher truth. Most styles are underpinned by eastern philosophies like Buddhism and Taoism which give the advanced students a path that leads beyond punching and kicking.

As you can see training and teaching martial arts addresses every aspect of human life and fulfils every one of the basic and advanced human needs. An involvement in this field offers an endless field of opportunities to help and grow, whether you are a total beginner or a seasoned master, whether you want to compete or reach enlightenment, whether you want to be in business or just have fun. In my view there is no other field of human endeavour that is as comprehensive and multi-faceted as the martial arts.

YOUR CORE BUSINESS

When asked to describe their purpose, a martial arts instructor, regardless of style and affiliation, will probably say that it is about teaching and educating newcomers to the martial arts, or instilling core values and life skills into children to give them a head start in life. I'm not disagreeing with any of that, but there is a fundamental difference between just teaching martial arts and running your own school. Running a school or academy, whether commercially or as a charity, is about much more than just spending time with your students and perhaps their parents.

When I started my first full-time school in Norwich a smart man once told me:

"You may be a black belt in your chosen style, but you are white belt in business." And how right he was! Pumped by excitement and enthusiasm I had romantic notions that all I had to do was to teach fun and exciting classes.

Well, that's only part of the story.

Like it or not, as martial arts professionals, we are essentially in the business of marketing and selling classes and courses. Teaching makes up only a small part in running a successful school. Instructors who do not realise this are systematically failing in running a successful, profit-making school.

It doesn't matter how good an instructor you (think you) are; if you don't have students you will only ever be a hobbyist. Being able to attract and keep students is a vital skill, which, in the context of business, I would even put above any martial arts skill. It makes really no difference if you are the next Bruce Lee if you can't sell the benefits of that to aspiring martial artists. The next step is of course keeping those students, which we will deal with later in this book.

I know a full-time school owner with over 250 students in the Midlands who got so busy with new students that he asked his brother to join him in his business. The problem was that his brother only ever dabbled in Karate/Kickboxing and up to that point was never even close to being a black belt. That didn't stop this enterprising school owner and he started to fast track his brother while at the same time getting him to teach the beginners class. All he had to do for the first year or so was to stay one lesson ahead of the class. I know that this doesn't seem very ethical to many, but it helps to illustrate an important point.

The truth of the matter is that running a successful school has very little to do with your martial arts abilities and everything to do with your ability to connect with potential clients so that they sign-up for your classes. Ultimately, your students don't really care how much you know, but they know how much you care. Don't make the mistake of judging other people by your standards. People start to train for their reasons and it is your job to make them stay for your reasons – to get to black belt.

IF YOU BUILD IT THEY WILL COME, WON'T THEY?

In 1989 Kevin Costner starred in the movie Field of Dreams. It's an all-American tale of a corn farmer who is a hard core baseball enthusiast who keeps hearing a voice that tells him: "if you build it they will come". For some reason he thinks that this voice is telling him to dig up his corn field and to build a baseball field. If he did this, he felt that certain famous but deceased baseball legends will come and play a game on his field. Being a Hollywood movie, that's of course exactly what happened and the corn farmer gets to play with his long-dead baseball heroes.

Although the plot seems quite ridiculous the "if I build it they will come" belief seems to be pretty widespread amongst inexperienced school owners.

Conducting entertaining classes and hoping that the classes will grow as the word spreads is simply not enough, especially if you have fixed overheads to pay, no matter how many students turn up (or not). It's quite simple, without paying students your dream of your own full-time school will quickly become a nightmare. Right from the word go you have to be aware that it is your job to get the word out there and make people aware that you exist and why they should be bothered to check you out. But that's not enough, once they are getting curious you have to sign them up. If you fail to do that you have wasted all your marketing efforts as well as their time on top of that. It doesn't really matter how strong your Kung Fu or how black your belt is, you will be gone in six months flat.

THE THREE AREAS OF YOUR MARTIAL ARTS BUSINESS

In the context of what I have outlined above it is important that you understand the actual teaching of martial arts classes only makes up around 30% of your daily workload, maybe even less if you are an established school with assistant and trainee instructors. This might seem to be an exaggeration, but teaching should really be one of the least of your worries. At this point, I am just taking it for granted that you have enough knowledge, experience and a curriculum to keep your students happy for at least the first year. The rest is divided into pro-active marketing activities and the back-office tasks like managing students and parents, phone calls, emails, bills, etc., which just keep accumulating. Please refer to the Martial Arts School Organisational Chart below.

In the same way that you should never go into a class without a lesson plan, especially as a new instructor, you should also plan your marketing and organisational activities well in advance and arrange your weekly timetable so that you allocate sufficient time to do the necessary things that you hate doing, like book-keeping for example. Please don't allow these things to accumulate and thereby put further strains on you.

Speaking from my own experience it is very easy to hide behind your desk and just do the things with which you are most comfortable. I think it is probably safe to say that most instructors I have meet are quite creative people, which can sometimes become a liability if you are busying yourself with yet another new poster design or fiddle around with your website instead of getting out there and getting new students.

Stop making excuses; it's your job, get on with it!

We will talk about this in more details later, but I would like to briefly explain why it is so important to be consistent, especially in your marketing activities. Many new businesses hit peaks and troughs throughout the year not so much because of seasonal fluctuations, but mainly because they make an effort and step things up when times are tough. However, once things seem to recover they stop with those things that helped them to improve the situation, only to find themselves back were they started. This very short sighted "crisis management and damage control" approach does not only cost you a lot of time and money, but ultimately puts your whole operation at risk, time and time again. It's a bit like paddling in a boat to get some momentum going and then stopping once you're gliding smoothly through the water, only to be forced to start paddling again because you've lost momentum.

> "I hate admitting this in print, but mediocre marketing with commitment works better than brilliant marketing without commitment. What makes marketing work? If you look for a one-word answer to that question, that would be commitment. What makes a marriage work? What makes a business work? How do you finish running a marathon? Commitment is the answer, and all the winners know it."
>
> **JAY CONRAD LEVINSON**

Once you are in a better position financially I would advise you to start outsourcing low value activities like cleaning, tax returns, etc.

WHAT TYPE OF BUSINESS WILL YOU START? PROFIT VS NOT PROFIT

"To confuse business with charity, is like a raising a vegetarian shark and then wonder why you're missing an arm and maybe even a leg."

TALIB FEHLHABER

There are a variety of ways to set-up and run your martial arts school, whether as a full-time centre or out of a church hall. The two biggest distinctions are if you want to run your school as a non-profit making charitable enterprise or as a business. Each is very different in the way it is set-up and has different tax implications, but there is not much difference in the way each should be run, if you want to make your school a long-term success story.

British comedian, Steve Coogan, once told a joke about footballer David Beckham, who is probably unlikely to win a Nobel Prize for physics: "They say, 'Oh, David Beckham—he's not very clever.' Yeah. They don't say, 'Stephen Hawking—shit at football.'"

Successful businesses are a bit like Mr Beckham. Both excel at one thing: in Mr Beckham's case, kicking a ball; in the case of a business, making profits. They might excel at other things too, but profitable businesses are successful because they focus on what they are good at. Be clear what it is you want to do with your school or club and don't get confused or side-tracked about your purpose and mission.

RUNNING A NON-PROFIT MAKING ORGANISATION

Just because you like to run your school as a non-profit making organisation, does not mean it's less bureaucratic or easier to run. In fact running a charitable organisation is probably a lot more bureaucracy-intensive than a humble sole-trader set-up.

If you want to run your school as a non-profit making organisation you have two options. First, you can register as a charitable organisation to get charitable status. There are over 180,000 registered charities in the UK at the time of writing. It is not as simple and straightforward as it was only a few years ago to get charitable status. In the UK you have to contact the Charity Commission and go through the application process. In order to set-up a registered charity you need to have a constitution, trustees, a secretary, a treasurer and have a minimum annual turnover of £5000 in order to be even considered for application.

You should really ask yourself if a charitable set-up is the best way for you before you start the application process, as you need to have regular committee meetings, which all have to be recorded and documented. There are annual elections of committee board positions such as secretary, chairman, treasurer, etc. You also need to file annual reports with the Charity Commission. My experience as a former secretary of a registered charity was filled with club politics and unnecessary bureaucracy, both of which I loathe. I'm not trying to put you off (completely) but you should be aware that this format is certainly not an easy option to run, set-up and administer your club.

For more information visit the website of the Charity Commission: www.charitycommission.gov.uk.

Another option is to set-up a Company Limited by Guarantee, which is also non profit. These are also known as guarantee companies.

In simple terms, a guarantee company is a not-for-profit company, and is the type most often formed by charitable organisations. A guarantee company does not have share capital, and the members do not own the company – they are decision-makers for the company, but do not receive any profits, and have no claim on the company's assets. All income generated is used to cover operating costs and to achieve the objectives of the company. In the event of the failure of the company, the liability of the company directors is limited to one pound.

RUNNING A PROFIT-MAKING BUSINESS

Amongst the more common ways of running your school there are mainly three different business formats. Sole trader, Partnership and Limited Company. As a one-man-band you probably will be starting out as a so called Sole Trader. I have used this legal format so far, as it is simple and needs no registration other than the notification to your local tax office, but it is also the type of business exposed to the greatest personal risk: as a sole trader, you are responsible for all aspects of the company, and have unlimited liability to all debts and legal actions. You may find it more difficult to attract outside investment or partners, which could hinder the expansion of the business.

As a sole trader you are effectively the business, for example Joe Bloggs trading as JB Martial Arts Academy. If the business were to fold with debts you would have to settle these debts from your personal assets. On the upside you get to keep all the profits you make and there isn't much in the way of paperwork except the inevitable regular book-keeping and your annual tax return.

Then there is the Partnership, which comprises two or more partners in the business. I wouldn't recommend this format at all especially not from the outset. The reason is simple; many business partnerships don't last very long and often end on a sour note, which could cost you some valuable friendships. You might want to consider this format later to attract some venture capital in order to expand operations and become a multiple school owner. But even then I would call for caution. There are just too many mismatched expectations and assumptions that could quickly become true kill-joys.

The third option would be to set-up a Private Limited Company (Ltd), which is still relatively straightforward and can be done for under £30 online.

A private limited company is a legal entity in its own right, separate from those who own it, the shareholders. The potential tax advantages and simplicity of running a private limited company make this the most common form of registered business in the UK. As a shareholder of a private limited company, your personal possessions remain separate (unless they are secured against the business for borrowing), and your risk is reduced to only the money you have invested in the company and any shares you hold which you have not yet paid for.

In addition to limited liability this form of company is also considered to be more prestigious by other companies and the general public due to its legitimate nature and the way important information is recorded at Companies House. It can be more expensive to secure the services of an accountant than it would be as a sole trader and as you have to submit your accounts to Company House every year, means that everybody can access them as public record. I believe it is key to keep your overheads and expenses as low as possible, especially during your first year of operation, regardless of how much start-up capital you think you have.

If you are thinking of securing bank loans be aware that banks will always look for personal guarantees from directors of small limited companies, thereby negating limited liability on banking debts. There are also some differences with regards to how you get paid as a Sole Trader as opposed to a limited company and how you get taxed on that. Basically, limited company directors are taxed on personal income from the business while the Sole Trader is taxed on his/her profits. Problems can arise when directors think of the company money as their own. Directors are also employees of the limited company and are required to operate Pay As You Earn Tax (PAYE), i.e. withholding a certain amount of the salary as income tax, national insurance contributions, etc.

I would recommend talking to an accountant to decide which set-up would suit you best.

There are also other limited company formats, such as Public Limited Company (plc) and Limited Liability Partnership (LLP), but these are rarely used if ever to set-up a local martial arts school.

Here is an overview of some of the pros and cons of each type of company type

Business Type Pros & Cons at a Glance	Sole Trader	Partnership	Ltd. Company
Minimum Set-up costs	●	●	
Higher accountancy costs			●
Credibility			●
Favourable tax			●
Favourable Pensions			●
Limited personal liability			●
Unlimited personal liability	●	●	
Public balance sheets			●
Personal PAYE			●
Tax deductable expenses	●	●	●
Claim own car as expense	●	●	
VAT	●	●	●
Flexible Structure			●
Financial Sourcing			●
Bureaucracy			●
Mileage Allowance			●

THE BUCK STOPS WITH YOU!

"Responsibility is the price of greatness."
WINSTON CHURCHILL

Regardless of whichever legal format you eventually choose it is vital to understand that *you are the business* and you are ultimately responsible for any and all decisions you make as well as for those that you neglect to make. In business, the only people who will remind you of your short comings are those to whom you owe money. There is a saying that if you think nobody cares about you just try not paying your bills for a while.

Failing to accept full responsibility for your operation is a sure-fire recipe for disaster and ultimate failure. It does not matter who did what, whether your equipment supplier screwed up an order, or your billing company double-charged a student, or a junior instructor was rude to a parent; it is your fault. You are the business and if it wasn't for you selling them equipment or asking them to sign an agreement this "mess" wouldn't have happened in the first place. At least this is how a student or a parent would see it. Accepting full and unconditional responsibility for all areas of your business is the first step to being a martial arts professional. Yes, you get all the blame but you also get to keep most of the money. Is it fair? No, of course not but this is not some kind of game were everybody has to treat each other with kid gloves and needs to respect your feelings.

If you find this difficult to digest then I would have serious reservations about you being tough enough to make it in business. Don't get me wrong, you don't need to be ruthless or hard-nosed, but there is a certain tenacity that is required in order to make it through many of the unexpected challenges that are lying in wait for you. It can be sobering to realise that you are in fact the only one who really cares whether or not you make it in business.

There is a great temptation for rookie school owners to shy away from certain areas of responsibility in the business and to outsource the things they don't enjoy or delegate them to members of staff. Again, delegation and outsourcing are great and important things and there will come a point in the life cycle of your school when you have to outsource certain things in order to grow. BUT my advice to a complete newcomer to running a martial arts school is don't do it, at least not straight away. Learn all aspects of your school first before your delegate them. This is particularly true for your book-keeping and the sales process. If you pass on your book-keeping too early, for example, there is a real risk that you might lose the bigger picture as to how your school is really doing. You might be spending money on things that do not give you any return on investment (ROI) or just haemorrhaging money without understanding why you have too much month left at the end of the money! [1]

The same is true for enrolling new students and upgrading existing ones. If you ain't doing it you can't expect anybody else to do it for you, and there is no one else to blame for it either, if your numbers are dropping off because you are too busy preparing for the next competition or improving your ground fighting skills. Remember the saying; "**If it is to be, it is up to me**".

Let me repeat that. It's vital that you keep a finger on the pulse of how your school is really doing, because if you choose to fly blind and inevitably crash there will be no one who will suddenly appear and miraculously rescue your business from failing. This is perhaps one of the single overriding reasons why many small school owners fail, because they expect someone else to sort out their problems.

---

1   Please refer to "E-Myth Revisited: Why Most Small Businesses Don't Work and What to Do About It" by Michael E. Gerber.

There is absolutely nothing wrong with asking for advice, but whatever you decide to do about it is your responsibility and you have to live with the consequences. There is no one to blame but yourself, this is what separates the wheat from the chaff and this is one of the key reasons why running your own business isn't for everyone.

"A man must be big enough to admit his mistakes, smart enough to profit from them, and strong enough to correct them."
JOHN C. MAXWELL

RAPID RECAP – KNOW YOUR BUSINESS

- Know what business you're really in – it's a lot more than just teaching people how to fight or compete.
- Realise business success has little to do with your martial arts ability – you may have a black belt in martial arts but if you're new to business you're a white belt entrepreneur.
- Understand the three areas of your martial arts business and how they relate to each other – get one out of balance and your business will struggle.
- Decide whether you're aiming for profit or not – and understand the implications of that choice.
- Be familiar with the pros and cons of various "legal" vehicles you can operate and choose the one that suits you best.
- Remember, when you start your own business the buck stops with you – so be prepared to take responsibility and take steps to guard against avoidable problems from the outset.

BRAND YOUR BUSINESS

CHOOSE YOUR NICHE

*"An expert is a person who has made all the mistakes
that can be made in a very narrow field"*
NIELS BOHR

Due to the broad appeal of the martial arts it is vital that you find
your niche; a specific area you focus on that distinguishes you from
any competitor in your area. For instance, if you enjoy the more
realistic aspects of the martial arts then become known as an expert
for that. If you are more into the traditional aspects, then be the
man/woman for that. Or if you get your kicks from tournaments,
then focus on that. The worst think you can do is to muddle it all
up and become Jack of all trades, Master of none. You will lose focus
and waste an awful lot of resources, the time and money you
probably can't afford to waste, on any number of "cool" things.
What's worse is that your students can't help but be mystified as to
what is expected of them.

But even in your own style and in your own school you need to
have clarity of purpose to avoid confusion. I know a very capable
BJJ instructor who couldn't make up his mind whether he wanted
to run a school, be a competitor or coach others to compete. The
inevitable result is that he did not manage to win any tournaments,
neglected his students as he had to train for own his fights and
hardly attracted any new students as he allocated very little time for
marketing. This confusion or lack of purpose creates frustration and
leads to mismatched expectations; the result of which is always that
people will lose out, get fed up and either quit or go somewhere
else.

Resist the temptation to go with the flavour of the month, whether it is MMA today, some type of military combat system (unless of course that is your system of choice) tomorrow, or any other "craze" that might come along next. Stick to what you are good at and what you enjoy the most, as it is your unrivalled passion for your art or style of choice that rubs off on your students. I have known capable Karate instructors who have embarrassed themselves in front of students because they felt that they needed to match the current demand for "ground 'n pound" and introduced Karate Ground Fighting. Another full-time school owner in the Midlands made me cringe when he revealed to me that, in an attempt to create greater appeal to his already quite respectable student base, he was teaching Escrima classes, based on "skills" he had learned from some recently purchased DVD's.

Don't try to be everything to everybody; you will simply dilute the essence of what makes you a great instructor. I have learned over the years that most people don't actually care what style or martial art you are teaching just as long as they are safe in the knowledge that they are training with someone who knows what he/she is doing and that he/she is willing and able to support them all the way to their training goal.

I am often reminded of a story I heard many years ago that illustrates this point beautifully.

There was an old man, a boy and a donkey. They were going to town and it was decided that the boy should ride.

As they went along they passed some people who thought that it was a shame for the boy to ride and the old man to walk. The old man and boy decided that maybe the critics were right so they changed positions.

Later, they passed some more people who thought that it was a real shame for that man to make such a small boy walk. The two decided that maybe they should both walk.

Soon they passed some people who thought that it was stupid to walk when they had a donkey to ride. The man and the boy decided maybe the best thing would be for them both to ride the donkey.

Not long after that, they passed a group who thought that it was a shame to put such a load on a poor helpless animal. The old man and the boy decided that maybe the critics were right so they decided to carry the donkey.

As they crossed a bridge, they lost their grip on the animal and he fell into the river and drowned.

The Moral of the Story: If you try to please everyone, you might as well kiss your ass goodbye!

Here are five solid reasons why you should become a widely known expert in your chosen area of expertise:

Elevated Status

You will elevate **your** own status by aligning yourself with other experts in your field.

Fewer Competitors

If you do what everybody else does there is very little that potential students can use to differentiate your services – apart maybe from price and you definitely want to stay out of price wars!

More Efficient & Focused Marketing

The beauty of a clearly-defined niche is that it focuses your marketing efforts like a laser beam and can cut down on a lot of useless and costly marketing spend.

More Referrals

Since you are operating in a clearly-defined niche, with little competition, others, including other martial arts professionals, will know to whom they can refer relevant students.

Adding Value

When you identify and understand your target audience, you can address the issues your students are looking for by helping them to get quality results fast, without diluting it with non-related distractions.

ASSOCIATIONS AND PROFESSIONAL BODY MEMBERSHIPS RELATED TO YOUR NICHE

There many different organisations in the UK that offer you an association as a fellow martial arts professional depending on the style your teaching, i.e. The British Judo Association, The British Karate Association, The British Council for Chinese Martial Arts, etc,.

Some of these are not much more than insurance brokers but others can provide quite a comprehensive service ranging from accredited curriculums to Dan grade recognitions and tournament organisation. As this industry is not regulated there is a fine balance between being your own man and bowing to the bidding of some organisation that might not even have any official recognition. It is definitely worth shopping around.

CHOOSING A BUSINESS NAME

"Nomen est Omen."

LATIN PROVERB, LITERALLY MEANING "NAME IS OMEN." IMPLYING THAT THE NAME IS FITTING OR EVEN THE DESTINY FOR THE OBJECT OR PERSON.

The name of your school represents, in many ways, who you are, what you stand for and to whom you wish to appeal. There are plenty of martial arts schools that are simply named after their owner, like "Master Smith's Martial Arts School of Excellence", or

"Sensei Cheng's Black Belt Centre". I called my first school "The Norwich Wing Tsun Martial Arts Academy of Excellence" which is a bit of a mouthful and fits on no stationery or cheque book, which I found out later. The reason for the name was that I was affiliated at the time to a particular group of Kung Fu schools and that name form was the common wisdom back then. I later changed the name to "The Rapid Defence Martial Arts Academy", because I felt that it reflected the ethos of what I wanted to teach; functional martial arts as opposed to competition or esoteric-based styles.

But with a view to the future I also wanted to avoid being tied down to a particular style, as I was still very much re-evaluating what I was teaching at the time. I also thought if I ever wanted to sell the business on to somebody it would be easier if it wasn't tied up with my name. But these are just some personal considerations and as long as you choose a memorable name that you think you can still live with in ten years time, then give it your best shot.

Once you have short-listed a couple of names run them past some friends, students and fellow instructors to get some feed back. If most of them can relate to and even remember a particular name, you're on to a winner.

I think there's a case to be made here to create as wide as an appeal as possible despite your specific niche, as most people can rarely distinguish between "Kung Fu" and "Karate". We have parents at our school, who have been bringing their kids to our (Kung fu) classes for years and still call it "Karate". Another consideration is how easily you can be found online, as most people would type in the first thing they associate with martial arts training, which is probably not your specific style.

A very useful tool that can assist you here is Google Trends (just type it into Google) which allows you to see which terms are being searched for the most compared to others. The graphic below shows that the search term "MMA" has historically been more popular than "martial arts" and "Karate", which is still one of the most popular styles in the UK. It is easy to see that the term "MMA" features high in the search engines because it receives a lot of press coverage. It has little to do with individuals searching for a local club to get fit. The broader the search-term however, the higher the search ranking, meaning that more people are using specific words to look for what you have to offer.

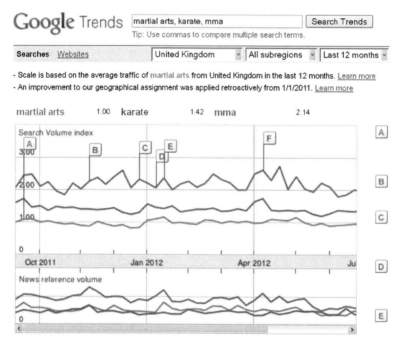

So if you have total freedom and are not necessarily tied too closely to a style or association then I would recommend you to be as user friendly as possible with your school name and avoid unnecessary foreign words that only mean something to you and other initiated students. As a personal preference, I wouldn't make it all about your name or person either as people tend to expect to see you in every class as you are the advertised product. But these might be the exact reasons why you want to choose a particular name for your school. In the end it is more about how well you promote that name and

BRAND YOUR BUSINESS

what people associate when they hear or read your school name. A word of caution: don't keep changing your school name around. This is especially so when advertising online. Once you have established a brand name that is associated with a certain image, key words and page rank it's a lot of work to bring the new name on par with the old one. This again might drain a lot of money and time that you could be otherwise spending much more productively.

DESIGNING OR CHOOSING A LOGO

Your school logo is your essence and your theme. Like your school name it should be something that resonates with you and your school ethos. Whatever you do avoid anything that could be construed as promoting or glorifying violence. Remember, most people choose to train in martial arts to get fit, not because they want to get kicked in the head or get slammed in to the mats, as much as this might seem strange to you now.

There certainly is an art to coming up with a good looking logo that reflects who you are without being cluttered with symbolism. If you don't mind spending some money you can search online for professional designers who are more than happy to come up with ideas for your logo, but it can be a lengthy process and there is no upward limit to how much you could end up paying and still not get what you are after. Trust your own creativity and vision and perhaps get some to help with making it look good.

Here are some ideas to help you design your logo. First choose a colour or colours that appeal to you. Remember that these colours have to somehow look right on your school uniforms and other paraphernalia. Go online and Google martial arts logos and then pick out a few that appeal to you. Print them out and write down what it is you like about them. Once you have a shape, colour and a symbol that rings your bell, you have the basics for a design spec.

Here are some basic logo design tips:

Simple Is Better
Keep your metaphor light, don't over clutter. It doesn't have to convey what your school does or what makes your style unique.

Size Matters
Remember that your logo has to be reproducible on any size from a billboard to a ball pen. Over complex logos don't resize well to a smaller size.

Your Logo Is For Your Audience
Just because you like or don't like a particular design doesn't mean you should or shouldn't use it. Understand what your audience likes and what you want them to associate with your logo when they see it. I was really shocked when I first saw that one of my students had my school logo tattooed on his arm. Not that I dislike tattoos, I just never imagined that my logo could prove so popular with students. Since then this has happened a number of times.

Strive To Be Different
When you do your online research you will see that there is a lot of the same when it comes to logos. Try to be unique by not over complicating things; you're not supposed to win a logo design competition.

Remember the K.I.S.S. rule, i.e. Keep It Simple Silly. More isn't necessarily better, it is just more and you want to avoid your logo looking cluttered and being difficult to be reproduced in print or in embroidery. Also, the more colours the more expensive it is to get it reproduced either as patches or directly onto your uniform and equipment. A tag line is fine but I wouldn't make that a part of your actual logo.

TRADEMARK

A trademark is simply anything that is unique to your business such as a word, combination of words, logo, colour, packaging or a personal name. It can cover a trade or a service and must be capable of distinguishing one company's goods and services from those of another. Your trade mark must not conflict with one already registered by someone else. Each trade mark application must specify the class of goods or services for which the registration is required. There are currently thirty-four classes of goods and eight classes of service to choose from.

Why Register A Trademark?
- To claim it as yours
- Helps raise brand awareness
- Enables brand extension into other products or markets
- Symbolise your quality
- To distinguish your business from competitors
- Prevent other businesses from copying your branding

A Trade mark can become a valuable asset, sometimes even priceless, such as Virgin and McDonalds. The Intellectual Property Rights of a business, in the form of its brand name(s), can be as valuable and important an asset as its bricks and mortar. Indeed in many cases it can be more valuable and critical to the survival of the business.

Trade mark registration acts as proof of ownership and entitlement to the brand, which entitles the owner to prevent competitors from using the same or similar trade marks on the same or similar goods.

The cost for registering your trademark is around £500, depending on how many classifications you chose.

RAPID RECAP – BRAND YOUR BUSINESS

- Choose a niche and join any associations you think will help you reach your target audience.
- Name your business for effectiveness, uniqueness, memorability and convenience.
- Logos should attract your target audience and say something, without words, about your business style and approach.
- Registering a Trademark is often a good idea – especially if you plan to franchise or license your idea in the future.

PLAN YOUR BUSINESS

*"In preparing for battle I have always found that plans are useless,
but planning is indispensable."*

DWIGHT D. EISENHOWER

Before we get into the nitty gritty of this section I have to come clean
with you. When I first started my full-time school, I did not have a
business plan or even a marketing plan. Although this doesn't make
me a bad person, with hindsight I can tell you now that this has cost
me time and money.

Like much of the information in this book I'm not trying to teach you
how to suck eggs. There are plenty of great books on how to write a
business plan. Although this might seem a daunting task it can really
work as a focusing tool and help you get some much-needed clarity to
keep you achieving your goals. I'm a great fan of outsourcing and even
the writing of a business plan can get done by others without great
expense. You can simply Google "business plan writing" to see what
kinds of deals are available to help you to prepare your business plan.
But as I warned you earlier about outsourcing book-keeping, getting
someone else to do this potentially removes you from the learning
curve. Make sure that you are involved at least in the key aspects of
conceiving the plan. After all would you allow a perfect stranger to
plan your next holidays for you?

But whichever way you go with that make sure that you DO get
one written. After you have some sort of a plan make sure that you
get an experienced pair of eyes to look it over for you. Plans are
based on assumptions that might not have any roots in (business)
reality. Remember, you don't want people to tell you what a great
job you did by coming up with a plan in the first place or how many
neat graphics or illustrations you use, but what the potential pitfalls
and misconceptions are, that you might have overlooked.

They love their acronyms and abbreviations in the military and it is hence no surprise that they should also have one when it comes to planning. It's called the six P rule. It goes as follows: Proper Preparation (or Planning) Prevents Piss Poor Performance.

And these guys should know as any unattended detail has the potential to jeopardise an entire operation at the cost of human lives. I like to use a military maxim here as most martial arts come from a military background and although it might not be quite so drastic in business life there is really no reason to waste your time and efforts – and those of others – because of an avoidable lack of planning.

So Who is Your Business Plan For?

Most people starting out on a business idea write some sort of business plan. I prefer to look at a business plan like mapping out a journey. No matter where you are planning to go you need a destination; some idea where you want to end up and of course how to get there.

To succeed in any kind of enterprise it is crucial to have a destination and a vision of where you wish your project to go. In the end it is not that important to actually get "there", as your priorities and circumstances may shift, but you need to have a sense of purpose that you are in fact taking your school somewhere.

The importance of having a destination is very well illustrated in one of my favourite novels. It is in "Alice in Wonderland" by Lewis Carroll. It's the famous scene where Alice meets the Cheshire Cat to ask for directions.

"Alice asks: 'Would you tell me, please, which way I ought to go from here.'
'That depends a good deal on where you want to get to,' said the Cat.
'I don't much care where – ' said Alice.
'Then it doesn't matter which way you go,' said the Cat."

It never ceases to amaze me that people spend more time planning their next annual holiday than planning any other aspect of their lives! Don't leave one of the most important ventures of your lives to chance. It will make the journey at least twice as hard, as you have to continuously re-assess your bearings, which makes you vulnerable to become easily side tracked. This can of course become costly, both in time and money.

Many think that a business plan is something with which to dazzle your bank manager or woo potential investors or partners, but I believe that the best business plans are written for the business founder.

They should give you a clear understanding of where the school is heading and how it is able to generate money. This clarity is almost priceless as it will help you avoid venturing into areas that you didn't plan for and perhaps shouldn't head into – at least not for now. It will keep you on course and will help you to overcome obstacles and setbacks.

There is a well-known saying: "Long-term goals can help to overcome short-term setbacks".

Your business plan should help you understand your business inside out and aid you as some kind of road map for the crazy times that lay ahead of you in your new venture. Problems arise when people try to write their plans backwards.

Some martial arts school owners start their business by obsessing over a calculator to work out how much money they need to make to be successful or to make ends meet and then work their way backwards. It is absolutely critical that you understand that you cannot make the figures fit your business, you have to allow the business to form the figures.

What I mean to say is that some school owners like to think about the size of their dojos or the kind of car they like to drive only to build a picture of a school that is very expensive to run. These expenses mean they have to sell a lot more memberships and equipment and hence create a business plan that predicts very high sales figures that bear absolutely no relation to what the market can realistically sustain.

It's like wanting to compete with the British Judo squad in the next Olympic Games and obtaining sponsorship on the false claims of an amazing skill-set whilst you have no training or experience at all.

These projections might look realistic on paper and some fledging school owners might even believe their own hype, but this can lead to some very sour grapes. The people they try to convince are often the people closest to them, such as their family and friends who might even invest in this dojo in the clouds, only to end up losing their hard-earned savings. I have known school owners who have collected much of their students training fees up-front and spent it in order to make their dream of driving a Ferrari come true. What they didn't realise was that they in fact stripped their school clean of its assets with very little motivation left to teach once the money was gone.

Go to the www.martialartsbusinessschool.com website to download a readymade martial arts business plan template, which will help you to have yours done in no time at all.

SWOT ANALYSIS

A SWOT analysis is a great analytical tool to figure out which areas of your business are the most vulnerable and which possess the greatest opportunities for growth.

SWOT stands for Strengths, Weaknesses, Opportunities and Threats. This little test can be applied to virtually any area of your school.

It is a very widely used template in all areas of business and education to get a better idea of where you are, what is playing in your favour and what could potentially trip you up. This is a

PLAN YOUR BUSINESS

particularly good and easy tool to use as you need to do a lot of planning before you set out on starting your own school and although you might be well aware of your strengths, you need to understand what your weaknesses are and how to turn threats into opportunities.

	HELPFUL to achieving the objective	HARMFUL to achieving the objective
INTERNAL ORIGIN attributes of the organisation	STRENGTHS	WEAKNESSES
EXTERNAL ORIGIN attributes of the environment	OPPORTUNITIES	THREATS

So following on from the classic rookie mistakes that you must avoid, here are my seven hard-earned survival tips for any aspiring and existing martial arts school owner.

1. Quo Vadis? – Know Where You Are Going

It is absolutely paramount that you know and understand why you want to start a martial arts school. This is important for a number of reasons, but most of all it can work as a life saver when the fertiliser hits the air conditioning and you start to lose focus. Once you are clear about what it was you set out to do, it is much easier to get your bearings back and to get back on track. I know I have mentioned it before and I don't mind saying it again, clarity is your very best friend, especially clarity of purpose.

2. No Surrender, No Retreat

There are so many parallels between the martial arts and making it in business, it is almost cliché. Many ancient war manuals like Sun Tzu's strategic manual "The Art of War" have been used by big business managers for decades.

And like any great general it takes a special someone to keep going when everybody is telling you to stop trying and to quit. As far as I am concerned simply quitting is completely unacceptable, not because of some misguided pride issue, but quitting is just too easy and what's more I know it in my bones that I will regret it later anyway.

> *"A man can fail many times, but he is not a failure until he begins to blame someone else."*
> **JOHN BURROUGHS**

The life of a martial arts school owner is full of unexpected twists and turns as well as some very nice rewards. Quitting is for people with a nine-to-five job, who keep blaming their boss or their colleagues for their misfortunes. Stop your jibbering and jabbering; it's your fault, own up and get on with it! The difference between a successful school owner and the opposite is that the successful man (or woman) got up that one more time.

3. You Are Who You Are With

Surround yourself with people who inspire you and motivate you to plough on. It is very easy to get dragged down by people with little or no ambition. Ask yourself, who you would choose to have with you in a fight. It might sound a bit harsh but you have to practice what I like to call "mental hygiene". If you want to stop smoking you can't be around smokers, who feel so guilty about their own addiction that they will give you cigarettes for free so you won't show them up.

I find it very refreshing from time to time to visit some of the hundreds of business conferences that take place all over the UK (mainly in London to be honest). These events are frequented by actual and aspiring entrepreneurs from all walks of life. It is quite inspiring to learn how some people, who would appear not to be the sharpest tools in the shed, are able to make an income from some weird and wonderful ideas. I suppose the danger is to get hooked on these events and to spend your hard earned teaching income on "the next seminar". And there's always a next seminar. A tip from someone who's been there, leave your credit card in your car or hotel room before attending these events as some conferences can be unbridled pitch parties with some very convincing sales people. You have been warned!

4. Keeping An Open Mind

Never be too proud to ask for help or advice. It can be quite lonely sometimes when running your own show and you can get bogged down by the day-to-day running of your school. It is only normal to share and discuss what's keeping you up at night.

Leaders are readers, as they say, this means that you need to constantly learn and grow as a professional. Use every opportunity to increase your horizon and if you don't like reading then start compiling your very own audio books library. It is so easy these days to listen to stuff when you are on the move or if you are waiting for something. Turn your car into a mobile university and start listening to success authors and motivational speakers whenever you can. Some of my favourite authors include Anthony Robbins and Brian Tracy. I have included a recommended reading list in the back of this book that should keep you going for a while.

Another important thing that could give you the edge is to get yourself a mentor. I'm sure that you must be concerned about the cost of that, and if you're not you are either loaded or deluded. These guys can be very expensive. But it could be well worth your while to have someone who can work as your sounding board especially if you are about to make some important decisions. Retired business owners or managers are often more than happy to lend you a helping hand, but as with everything you get what you pay for.

5. Targets We Set Are Targets We Get
This might perhaps smell a bit too "salesy" to you, but there is nothing quite like hitting targets that you have set for yourself. In the end business is all about the numbers and the key to succeeding with those numbers is self-discipline. Set yourself realistic and achievable targets and then work until you hit them. Once you have done rinse and repeat.

You have to be self motivated when in business and nothing gets you back in the dojo on a bad day like the knowledge that your bank account is full and healthy, even on a cold, wet and windy day (of which there are many in the UK). Yes, you've guessed it, the opposite is true as well and if you can't even pay your bills it is very hard indeed to come across as confident and enthusiastic to your students. And as you are the "product" it just became a bit less fun to be with you.

6. Monitor, Measure And Adapt
You can't manage what you can't measure. Become a friend of numbers. Keep close tabs on all areas of your business. Frequently analyse how you are doing and where you are heading and if necessary fine tune and adapt your goals and strategies. Performance that is monitored effectively will serve you as an early warning system, that can help you make the right decisions at the right time.

Instead of an ongoing learning curve, many school owners that I have met seem to have several one-off twelve-month experiences and are happy to keep repeating the same mistakes year after year.

This is a clear indicator that they do not measure their results and then learn from them.

For example: School owner Master Matt Burns knows that August can be a quiet time for recruitment due to the long school summer holidays. This became painfully evident in the hit he took in his enrolments the year before around that time. Instead of planning for that bottleneck, twelve months on, by either doubling his marketing efforts the month before or to embrace it by offering specific martial arts summer camps, for children and/or adults, he gets stung by another lull in his enrolments, which he feels even more due to the average monthly attrition. This in turn adds additional stress and money worries, all due to an avoidable lack of planning.

DID YOU KNOW?

About 50% of all your marketing is a complete waste of time and money; the trick is to figure out which half to avoid.

Keep a diary of all planned, as well as unplanned, marketing activities. Record what returns you get from specific campaigns; for example, how many enquiries and enrolments each and every ad or leaflet brought you. Consult this diary to make next year's planning easier and to help you to eliminate a lot of the guess work that much of marketing is. Another common mistake is to outsource your book-keeping too early just because you don't like doing it. It is very important to keep a finger on the pulse and to know where your money is going. Especially at the early stages, it is vital to understand and learn what could be siphoning off your hard earned money and stopping you becoming profitable. You need to have a feel for keeping things on an even keel, before you can think about passing it on to someone else.

7. Love Your Students

Without a loyal student base your school will not succeed. Focus on building lasting relationships and always respond quickly when your customers complain or point out something that could be improved. In today's world it is all about the customer's experience and people will talk about you via social media, so your best bet is to embrace it. Become internet savvy and learn how to use things like Facebook and Twitter to your advantage. Remember: people don't care how much you know, but they know how much you care.

ESSENTIAL LEGAL REQUIREMENTS

The martial arts industry is largely unregulated in the UK and therefore anybody can set-up a club or school without fulfilling any specific legal requirements. However there are some professional standards to which you should commit, not only to set yourself apart from the competition but also to plan more long-term.

CRB Checks

All instructors at my school are CRB checked and although this might be something that could well change again in terms of legislation, it shows that you are 'legit' and take your students' welfare seriously. The same applies to First Aid qualifications, there should be at least one fully qualified first aider at your school while classes are in progress. Following the US, Old Blighty is increasingly becoming a litigious society and not being able to at least say that you could have helped if and when a student or visitor injures themselves, could potentially shut down your operation permanently. Not a legal requirement (yet) are child safety procedures and relevant training, which can be obtained very easily via the web. Check out www.safechild.co.uk which provides CRB checks as well as online training courses for child protection. Again, a real plus if you intend to teach children and vulnerable adults in your club.

Insurance

I hope that it goes without saying that everybody in your school, who has any student interaction, needs to be fully insured (OK, maybe not the receptionist). All instructors must have their instructor's indemnity insurance and the trainees need their member to member insurance, which insures them against each other. As the business owner you need to have some public liability insurance as well. Don't wait or put your insurance cover off for later as there are two types of people when it comes to insurance. There are those who have sufficient cover and then there are those who wish they had. Just because your previous school didn't have one or the other should not be a reason for you to skimp on insurance cover, as this could spell sudden death for your school owner ambitions.

Apart from the necessary training and teaching qualifications all our instructors are fully insured, fully qualified first aiders, qualified in child safety and fully CRB checked. Although you are not legally required to have any of these I believe every instructor should be made to have them all, which goes a long way in making your students and their parents feel safe in the knowledge they have come to a professional outfit that takes its responsibilities for its members and staff seriously. If more school owners would think like this, it would seriously raise the standard of our industry and hopefully flush out some cowboys. But whatever everyone else is doing (or not) in the end shouldn't be your concern, just make sure you are beyond reproach.

Health And Safety

As I indicated above, the welfare of your students must be of paramount importance to you. Not just as a customer care exercise but also for legal reasons, because you as the business owner have a duty of care.

Certain responsibilities change depending on your set-up, such as whether you operate out of a Church Hall or Community Centre or out of your own premises. If you are lucky enough to call four walls and a roof your own school then you need to have some additional basics covered.

Health and Safety rules stipulate certain conditions when you open your place up to the public. Fire safety rules are especially important; not least because you might well get inspected by your local council for compliance.

In October 2006 the Regulatory Reform (Fire Safety) Order 2005 came into effect and replaced over seventy pieces of fire safety law.

The Regulatory Reform (Fire Safety) Order 2005 applies to all non-domestic premises in England and Wales, including the common parts of blocks of flats and houses in multiple occupation (HMOs). The law applies to you if you are:

- responsible for business premises
- an employer or self-employed with business premises
- responsible for a part of a dwelling where that part is *solely* used for business purposes
- a charity or voluntary organisation
- a contractor with a degree of control over any premises
- providing accommodation for paying guests

Under the Regulatory Reform (Fire Safety) Order 2005, the responsible person must carry out a fire safety risk assessment and implement and maintain a fire management plan. In order to find out what you need to do when carrying out a risk assessment you can download a five-step fire risk assessment checklist from the www.martialartsbusinessschool.com website.

Go to the Business Link website to get more detailed advice and guidance on the implementation of a fire risk management plan. Ensure that:

- All required emergency exit signs are displayed.
- Everybody knows where your assembly points are.
- You have sufficient fire extinguishers visibly displayed, easily accessible and in working order.

Fire extinguishers need to be serviced and if necessary replaced every year and refilled after use. Any local company specialising in fire extinguishers, etc. can advise you regarding current legal requirements.

A class roster would be a prudent idea in the case of a fire to check that everybody got out in time, but properly kept attendance cards could also do the trick. If your place has a fire alarm system it needs to be tested regularly and I would recommend recording those tests in a separate booklet or diary.

You also need to be prepared for emergencies that require First Aid. I mentioned before that there needs to be a qualified first aider at your school or class, so if you run as a one-man-band this means you. That means that if you are not yet a qualified First Aider, search out a local provider, like the St. John's Ambulance or the British Red Cross and get certified. You need a fully stocked First Aid kit in your bag or at your school, which also needs to contain an accident book to record any training related incidents. Please be aware that accident records fall under data protection and should not be openly available to anyone else at the school or class.

If you have your own premises in the UK you also need to display non-smoking signs.

Toilet facilities need to be adequate. This means that they need to be clean and accessible. You don't have to have separate toilets for men and women but they need to have a lockable door. There should be a good supply of toilet paper and for female trainees and staff a way to dispose of sanitary dressings.

Toilets are in many ways the most important facility in your school as everybody has to use them. You would be surprised how many people will judge your professionalism by the state of your toilets. How many times have you shared stories of some, shall we say, "less than adequate" facilities?

Disabled facilities are a bit of a grey area as the number of disabled people training in martial arts is very low. If you have any specific questions regarding that please feel free to contact the Disability Martial Arts Association (www.disabilitymartialartsassociation.co.uk).

Contracts

As the UK has unfortunately followed the USA in becoming an increasing litigious society where some companies act like vultures in proactively hunting down any accident that could possibly lead to a liability claim, you need to safeguard yourself, your students and your business. Apart from the necessary insurance that you must have, I would also advise you to use a liability waiver that every new trainee or guest must sign before any training takes places. I use a Student Profile Questionnaire that every newcomer needs to fill in and sign when they come for an induction or trial session. This also includes a disclaimer that resolves any and all fellow trainees and/or instructors and staff from any responsibility should that person injure him/herself. Given the nature of the activity (punching, kicking and/or throwing each other) it might be a little tricky to argue malice but accidents do happen and some people might like to take their chances. In almost twenty years of teaching martial arts and self-defence skills I never had anybody trying to take me or a fellow student to court over an injury.

You can download a Profile Questionnaire from the KickStart website, www.martialartsbusinessschool.com, which you can customize to your requirements.

RENTING/BUYING PERMANENT PREMISES VS SETTING UP IN LOCAL CHURCH HALLS, SCHOOLS OR LEISURE CENTRES

There are different ways of running a full or part-time martial arts school or club when it comes to the actual premises. I like to mention three ways through which you can run a profitable set-up. They all have their pros and cons and are really not better or worse than one another, they are just different and suit different needs.

You can run a school either by roaming, renting or buying a premises or a hall.

Roaming:
Roaming is quite common for travelling instructors who look after more than one club or branch. It can be relatively temporary in set-up and offers a lot of flexibility in taking your school to your students especially if they are children.

In this configuration you would hire a venue by the hour, which is your typical church hall or community centre set-up. This method tends to work well in rural areas, like in Norfolk where I live, where many kids simply wouldn't be able to do any martial arts training if it wasn't for their instructor coming to their village or town. I know several instructors who travel as far as fifteen miles in different directions from where they live to service various locations.

The obvious advantage of this mobile set-up, is that it provides a massively enhanced catchment area to the instructor. It offers a great convenience factor for students and parents, which can go a long way in ensuring student loyalty.

The disadvantages include the obvious additional fuel costs and wear and tear to a car or a van, not to mention the time spent driving to various venues. All equipment such as pads, gloves and weapons needs to be hauled around, as it is needed at each location to keep costs down. If you have classes twenty to thirty strong, that can be a lot of equipment! If you do any grappling art like Judo you also have to plan for additional time to set-up and tidy away your mats. Any merchandise that you might want to sell, such as clothing and equipment, also needs to travel. It might not be straightforward to display any or all of these items, which can make them slow to sell.

Renting:
This way is similar to the roaming version but might not involve that much travelling if you focus on a particular location. I started teaching in just such a church hall, which I hired twice a week. It is a great way to build up a student base before committing to a dedicated place, as it keeps your overheads low. Apart from the other certifications, like CRB checks, insurance, etc. which you should have regardless, it frees you from any responsibility for bills and cleaning. But as with roaming you might have to still bring all your equipment and wares and set-up every time from new.

The alternative is that you find something more permanent that you can customise and perhaps even sub-let while you are not using it.

This would be the renting or leasing option of a property, which can be a shop, warehouse or even some converted office space. Although you can easily become a full-time instructor without a dedicated venue this option is perhaps the most common form of setting up a full-time school. A dedicated place that bears your name and logo is a very special step-up as you become an established feature in your community; you could almost say an institution!

There are different ways that you can rent or lease premises, but before you sign on the dotted line please find out the rateable value of the premises. This is the council tax equivalent for a business (which doesn't even get you your rubbish collected, at least not in Norwich). Contact the Valuation Office or your local council for details. The rateable value of a commercial property is re-evaluated every seven years by the Valuation Office and is either lowered or increased. The local council merely collects this tax.

After nearly five years in the premises that we are currently in, the Valuation Office kindly re-evaluated the property and hit me with a £5000 back dated bill for business rates, which had to be paid back over ten months. As you can imagine this ate quite a bit into my bottom line, but "luckily" was tax deductible. A bit of research hence makes a lot of sense, at least to help you avoid surprises like that.

Also, make sure that your local council would be prepared to consider a change of use from the existing, for your intended school, if needed. More about that later.

The great thing about having a place to call your own is that it will give you a lot more kudos and credibility than being in a local church hall. You can lay out the school and customise it to your preference, including a reception, changing rooms and showers, a dedicated Pro-Shop, etc. I have visited a number of dedicated schools which also have a gym area with machines and free weights. It's a good idea if you have the space, as it gives students another reason to stay.

The commitment of a full-time place naturally brings a lot more responsibilities, like bills, insurances, maintenance, etc. The way your school looks and is kept is very much a reflection of your own dedication and professionalism. Make sure to keep on top of it.

Buying:
Owning your own commercial property is a big step particularly if you are only starting out. The advantages and responsibilities are very similar to that of a leased or rented property, but you are far more tied to the venue and if things don't work out it's not easy to just walk away. On the other hand you might view a property as an investment which might give you some income at a later stage through rent or by selling it off at a profit. Be careful about the mortgage deal you are offered, as interest rates in the UK are currently at a record low level and can only go up.

DEALING WITH LANDLORDS

Once you have a venue you need to know how to deal with your landlord. I would initially be careful in signing any lengthy lease even if you get the first six months rent free to do the place up. Recent changes in legislation have forced landlords to pay business rates even if the premises are vacant. This means that many landlords are very keen to fill any vacant business premises in order to avoid haemorrhaging money in taxes and having to keep the properties in good nick for prospective tenants. Understanding this puts you in the driving seat when it comes to negotiating your terms, but be careful; if the deal sounds too good to be true it often is. Check with your local council if any surrounding or adjacent buildings are due for demolition or redevelopment, which can cause you untold hassle and a drop off in business as building work takes place next door. Also make sure that your own building hasn't got planning permission to be turned into a car park or town flats. It is often what your landlord doesn't tell you that is the most interesting and revealing. Ask around in the neighbourhood, many local business owners are quite well informed as to what goes on in their neck of the woods.

Some landlords and/or their agents can be quite shrewd sales people and might try to pressure you into a rash decision that you will later regret, by telling you that they have several other interested parties or that the deal will expire in the next seven days.

When it comes to spending money and hiring people *always* take your precious time.

Once you have secured a good venue at a decent location make sure to renegotiate your lease as often as possible if you have a short-term lease. The end of the year is often a good time to approach your landlord as they don't like the prospects of rental voids it might not necessarily get you a discount or rebate, but if you don't ask you don't get. Doing the place up and keeping it well maintained also gives you more bargaining power, but be careful not to go crazy with renovation and interior decorations if you only have a short-term lease on the place. If you have entered a long-term lease contract there is not much you can re-negotiate, unless something has happened to the building, like fire or water damage.

Business Rates

Please also bear in mind that the rent or lease is only a part of the cost you might face. Apart from your monthly energy and phone bills all commercial premises in the UK are individually taxed via business rates, which in some cases could double the cost of your lease or rent. Business rates are public record and you can easily find out via your local council what rates may apply for the particular premises you are interested in.

If you own a small business which has a rateable value of below £18,000 a year (or less than £25,500 in Greater London) you could claim up to half of your business rates back with the money being paid by the Chancellor of the Exchequer. This will help you to stay profitable when business isn't great or when you are just starting out.

The UK Government has temporarily doubled the level of relief available. Between 1 October 2010 and 31 March 2013, eligible ratepayers will receive small business rate relief at 100 per cent on properties up to £6,000 (rather than 50 per cent), and a tapering relief from 100 per cent to 0 per cent for properties up to £12,000 in rateable value for that period.

The temporary Small Business Rate Relief increase will therefore apply throughout the whole of the 2012-13 billing year (until 31 March 2013). The relief was originally doubled by the government until September 2011, but this was extended by the Budget in March 2011, and then extended again in the 2011 Autumn Statement to take account of economic conditions.

Small business rebates are awarded via your local council and recalculated every year. You are only eligible for a rebate for one business premises at one time. Contact your local council or whoever your local billing authority is and put in a claim for rate relief as soon as possible.

Planning Permissions

Another thing to consider are planning permissions. Many, if not most, commercial units have an authorised use as a retail or workshop premises. It's it vital that you find out what the local planning department thinks about your idea to change the use of the place, BEFORE you sign a lease agreement. My experience from speaking to other instructors and school owners is that many local councils are a pain in the back side and are often quite resistant to changing the current use of a retail unit to anything else. This could mean that you might end up in a lengthy appeal process with your local council about the change of use, which can be costly if you then also have to engage surveyors, architects and solicitors to get your application approved. You can of course risk it and not inform your council of the change of use (but still pay your rates), if you get away with it unchallenged for seven years they will have to accept the new status quo. This is called a Certificate of Legal Use and is issued by your local Planning Department.

It's a pain considering that successive governments keep promising to boost small and medium sized business by reducing the red tape involved. If it makes you feel any better, in Germany, for example, this would be seen as an almost laughably small amount of bureaucracy considering the hoops entrepreneurs have to jump through when trying to set-up their own businesses. I hear also that the US isn't exactly what you what would call the land of opportunity anymore.

WHEN TO OPEN YOUR DOORS FOR BUSINESS

Following from what was mentioned in earlier chapters about the "If I build they will come" attitude, I would first recommend you generate some lively interest in your classes and hit the ground running by starting with a group of beginners. Not only does it look much better for any unexpected new arrival, as nobody wants to be the first and maybe even only one, in a new class or course. I would even go so far as offering your classes for free for the first ten students to create a class feel and to reassure newbies that they have come to the right club. You can always upgrade these first few to a higher programme later to make back your money. We will talk about upgrades a little later in this book.

Your best bet here is the internet again to announce your new courses or classes but don't put all your eggs into one basket. Most of your marketing efforts will probably end up driving traffic to your website, which is a good thing – providing that you have one that is.

A great way to recruit new students is to do good old public demos. People are exposed to martial arts moves in movies, television series and video games all the time these days, so showing off some moves will certainly get you the attention you need.

A word of caution here, please make sure that you and your helpers, if you have any, are properly instructed as well as fit enough to do the required routines. It's also crucial that you have sufficient insurance cover if something should go wrong, especially with members of the public. Do not under any circumstances invite any onlooker to take part in your demos or get talked into including some guy who fancies himself, unless it's part of your routine to have a hidden crew member posing as a spectator. As I mentioned earlier, Britain is the sad leader of yet another embarrassing European league table when it comes to liability suits. Some people are just gagging for the opportunity to take a gullible martial arts enthusiast like yourself to court to make a few thousand pounds out of you.

One of your team members (even if it's your mum) should go around to hand out promotional flyers or postcards and even take the names and contact details of interested punters. Make sure to tailor your demos to a specific audience. This could be a weapons demo for adults or a self defence demo for women or even a kids' class promotion if you have any children in your class you could borrow. You should try to look as professional as possible, so get everybody wearing your school T-shirt or hoodie.

Depending on your budget and time constrains, you should put up posters in shops and pubs and hand out flyers in the high street, even if it's just at the weekend.

Once you have around ten to twenty people on your waiting list you then announce the opening of your class in a press release to your local paper, as well as on Facebook. Make a big deal out of it and if possible invite anybody and everybody to come along. If you live in a small town you should defiantly try to ask your local mayor or the headmaster of the local school to come along. This can then be used in your press release to make it somehow newsworthy. There are really no limits to your creativity when it comes to shamelessly promoting yourself. And remember to ask everybody for a referral until they give you one!

RAPID RECAP – PLAN YOUR BUSINESS

- You need targets so you know where your business is going.
- Understand the strengths and weaknesses inherent in your proposed business and plan to guard against threats and capitalise on opportunities.
- Be aware of your legal responsibilities and cost / prepare for them appropriately.
- Decide on your location strategy – this may change as your business grows but set out with the right plan in mind.
- Know what needs to be in place before you open your doors for business and set a "launch date" to keep progress on track.

BONUS CHAPTER: HOW TO SURVIVE YOUR FIRST YEAR

"Prepare for bad times and you will only know good times."
ROBERT KIYOSAKI

If some popular business statistics are to be believed then 50% of all start up businesses fail within the first twelve months of their inception. Of those that survive, another 80-90% don't make it through the next five years. However, it has been suggested that these figures were actually compiled by people trying to sell franchises – go figure.

As Winston Churchill is quoted to have said:

"I only believe in statistics that I doctored myself"

With the start of your business it is inevitable that you will screw up regularly and in many different areas, but that's OK, it is how we learn. The trick is to make survivable mistakes.

I have already mentioned the top ten rookie mistakes earlier on, but there are many more things that can go wrong without really trying. Here are the five most common mistakes which cause many new martial arts schools to go bust:

1. Starting For The Wrong Reasons
Many a determined black belt wants to go it alone because he or she wants to make loads of money, or perhaps you like to spend more time with your family and children. Well, if that's why you want to start a school please think again. Don't get me wrong; there is definitely money to be made by teaching martial arts full-time, but

that should not be your primary focus. Also bear in mind that at least in the early stages you will be spending a lot of time away from your friends and family.

2. Poor Management

Most martial arts professionals frequently lack relevant business and management expertise in areas such as finance, purchasing, marketing, selling and hiring and managing employees. The good news is that reading this book should equip you with some of these skills or at least point you in the right direction so you can skill-up quickly.

3. Insufficient Capital

A common fatal mistake for many struggling martial arts schools is to have insufficient operating funds. Would be school owners underestimate how much money is needed and they are forced to close even before they have had a fair chance to succeed. Some may also have an unrealistic expectation of incoming revenue from memberships and sign-ups.

It is crucial that you understand how much money you will require; not just to getting started but also consider the costs of staying in business, like advertising budgets and unexpected expenditures. It is further important to take into consideration that you school may take a year or two to get going. This means you will either need enough funds to cover all costs, or your marketing efforts need to bring in the required results.

4. Lack of Planning

I've already mentioned this earlier, when I talked about business plans. If you were ever in charge of planning a successful event you will know that if it wasn't for your careful, methodical, strategic planning – and hard work – success would not have followed. The same could be said of most business successes.

5. No Website

A well planned and well designed website is an absolute must if you want your school to succeed in today's market. Gone are the days when people would pick up a chunky copy of the Yellow Pages to find you. The fact that you have an online strategy – at least a website that it is ranked on the first page of Google – can make all the difference between a school full of students or the alternative. This has absolutely nothing to do with how good you are as an instructor, if people can't find you or are not captivated by your online presence you are in for a challenge to say the least.

DID YOU KNOW?

80% of people who could be interested in training with you don't know that you exist.

It is also helpful to manage your expectations with regards to what can realistically be achieved within the first twelve months of operation. If you are breaking even within or after twelve months you are in fact doing a great job! It takes at least three to five years for a business to get established. Being forewarned on the classic pitfalls gives you a valuable edge over the competition, but it shouldn't make you complacent. When it comes to the success of your school, you – the business owner – are ultimately the "secret" of your success. For many successful martial arts school owners, failure was never an option. Armed with drive, determination, and a positive mindset, these individuals view any setback only as an opportunity to learn and grow. Most self-made millionaires possess average intelligence. What sets them apart is their openness to new knowledge and their willingness to learn whatever it takes to succeed.

PART TWO

DOING THE BUSINESS

ATTRACTING STUDENTS

*"Marketing is too important to be left
to the marketing department."*

DAVID PACKARD

As mentioned before we, as school owners, are first and foremost in the business of marketing and selling martial arts classes and courses. We do this predominantly via genuine and lasting relationships with our students and not through clever marketing ploys.

However, when I speak to school owners and instructors about marketing I hear different things from different people. Some think it's all about advertising others say it's about producing posters and leaflets or attending networking meetings. Whilst none of them are really wrong it does however highlight a common misunderstanding when it comes to marketing. To be crystal clear about what I mean by marketing in this book, I would like you to consider the following quote by Peter Drucker.

"The aim of marketing is to know and understand the customer so well the product or service fits him and sells itself."

In other words if you take care of your marketing in a dedicated and consistent way your sign-up rate will take care of itself.

This is one of *the* key aspects of running a successful full or part-time school. Many aspiring school owners fall short of ensuring proper and consistent marketing, which places them in a constant financial roller coaster.

You can be the best at what you are doing in terms of your chosen martial art, but if you have no students, or too few of them, it is both demoralising and financially risky, as even a small drop-off can have catastrophic consequences for the future of your school. I have met some school owners who try to justify their lack of students with the argument that quality and quantity are mutually exclusive, which is of course nonsense.

If that was the case then how do you explain the very tangible results of military organisations, which churn out thousands of experts in various specialist fields every year? The same is true for any university, diplomat or dance school.

Don't get me wrong; I'm not trying to persuade you to open up the next McDojo chain, but please consider that your personal standards belong only to you and if every educational institution settled only for absolute perfection from its students, as do some martial arts schools, then hardly anyone would get their A-levels or diplomas. To judge everyone by your (black belt) standards isn't just unfair to your students, but is also narrow minded.

"Every master was once a disaster." T. Harv Eker

In the same vein you can't take credit for your few outstanding students because they probably would have been good at whatever they tried. If you want to take credit for the good ones then you must also take credit for the much bigger portion of average and below average students.

Your standards are what they are, but if they inhibit you and the growth of your organisation then you have to seriously question them.

As full-time school owners we really have to be able to juggle three jobs at the same time. We need to teach, market our business and manage our school/club. Allowing any of these aspects to slide will put your entire operation in jeopardy.

Effective marketing, like learning and teaching martial arts is not an event, but an constant, deliberate and ongoing process. Attracting new students needs good planning and pig-headed discipline. But it is not enough just to be busy; you have to be doing the right things at the right time. In other words, to do more of the things that work and less of those things, that do not. This begins by knowing where you need to be at a specific point in the future. To say that you like to be busier or wealthier is merely stating a preference it becomes a plan once a time limit is attached to it.

In his book "The Seven Habits Of Highly Effective People" (which is a must read for you and should hold a special place in your ever growing business library) Stephen R. Covey talks about starting with end in mind.

"To begin with the end in mind means to start with a clear understanding of your destination. It means to know where you're going so that you better understand where you are now and so that the steps you take are always in the right direction. It's incredibly easy to get caught up in an activity trap, in the busy-ness of life, to work harder and harder at climbing the ladder of success only to discover its leaning against the wrong wall. It is possible to be busy – very busy – without being very effective."

It is extremely important that you have a clear understanding of where you want to be as a school and as an instructor.

I remember back in the day when I had to attend those dreaded job interviews, during which some smart Alec would inevitability ask me: "And where do you see yourself five years from now?" Looking back at this now I must say that this is actually not such a bad question if you don't want to find yourself just "anywhere" in a few months or years.

THE THREE RS OF MARKETING

Before we zoom in on the various aspects of marketing to ensure the maximum exposure and the best return on investment (ROI) with as many sign-ups as you can handle, I'd like to introduce you to the three Rs of Marketing.

These illustrate that there are basically three aspects to your effective martial arts marketing. These are:

- **Recruitment** – in many ways this is the life blood of your school or club. You need to understand that students come and go and it's therefore a constant and ongoing marketing effort to attract newbies to enrol with you.

- **Retention** – it clearly is not enough to just keep enrolling new students whilst not being able to hold on to them for any length of time and haemorrhaging them with a vengeance. Read more in the chapter on Customer Service on how to get a grip on that.

- **Recall or reactivation** – From a cost per student perspective this can be a cheap source of return custom to you if only you keep track of who is coming and leaving. People leave for their own reasons and unless that reason was you, they might like to resume their training in the future.

But before we start let's just ask; how many students do you really want or need?

I passionately believe that what I have to offer to my students is special and of a high value. In order to create a loyal student base I need to be able to consistently provide that high level of quality throughout. This of course becomes more challenging the more students I accept into my school, which to a point, is a problem you would want to have. The solution is quite straightforward. Unless I have several instructors working for me, I would rather have 100 students paying me £70 per month than 200 students paying me £35. The end result, which is an income of £7,000 per month, maybe the same but you halve the amount of potential problems and cancellations if you only have around 100 students.

Why do I keep talking about 100 students? I appreciate that for some of you reading this, it's an almost astronomical figure. But, believe me when I tell you that it is really not that hard to crack the magic number if you follow my advice in this book. Why? Because I've done it and if I can, so can you.

A hundred students is also a good target at which to aim and once you have reached it you know that you are now in the top 10% of martial arts school owners and that you have a relatively secure income that allows you to focus on the things you enjoy and like to do, as opposed to only the things you have to do in order to survive. Remember: Goals we set are goals we get. And even if you do fall short of that magic three digit marker, having "only" 80 students is not to be frowned at, especially if they pay well.

MARKETING VS. PUBLIC RELATIONS (PR) AND COMMUNITY RELATIONS

*"Some are born great, some achieve greatness
and some hire public relation officers."*

DANIEL J BOORSTIN

The job of marketing your business is to secure a constant flow of new students. Public relations, done right, on the other hand can help your business to gain credibility and to establish the branding of your corporate identity. This means that people will associate a service or message when they hear or see your logo, website or name. Names or brands like Nike, Dell or MacDonald's instantly evoke a picture and expectation all due to years of constant PR and advertising. If you are not what people associate with "martial arts" and your location then something else will.

Public Relations activities include community relations, publicity, membership in certain clubs and organisations and networking. If nothing else, publicity will put your name in the public eye. However, you want to be known and recognised for the right reasons, so don't get tempted by the saying that "Even bad publicity is good publicity as long as they spell your name right."

Community Relations is perhaps the more altruistic side of your marketing. Joining clubs and organisations with the distinct intention to show how dedicated you are to your local community seems somewhat self-serving, but you would be surprised how many do it. Being involved in serving your community can help to get you some powerful contacts, especially if you invest a lot of time and energy without serving your business interests first. There is a certain attraction for potential students and their families if they can see that you are busy working in and for the community without getting paid. It shows that you care.

One example of community relations that will undoubtedly generate a lot of goodwill and great publicity for you is to get your members to clean up litter at a local park or playground. All you need is a few bin bags a camera and a press release. Activities such as these also help to create a greater bond inside your school amongst the students and parents, as they will begin to feel to be part of a force for good.

A few carefully placed activities like that throughout the year will continue to give people something positive to talk about you. This will become part of your Referral Engine once done consistently.

So now that we've cleared that up, let's examine actual marketing a little closer. Martial Arts marketing, is divided into internal and external marketing. Both are equally important and must be planned and practised with equal consistency and diligence.

External marketing covers all activities that are aimed at providing you with the much needed fresh blood of new beginners in your school.

Here are fifty-five tried and proven things you can use to boost your student numbers:

Online tools such as your:
1. Website (with privileged members section)
2. Landing pages. (one page websites for special offers and promotions)
3. Facebook Fan page(s)
4. Google Places. (a free way to get you to the top of Google searches in your town or area)
5. YouTube Channel
6. Twitter account
7. LinkedIn account. (a great place to connect with business minded people.)

8. Pinterest.com
9. Ads in online free papers like Gumtree, etc.
10. Google Adwords. (use sparingly and targeted to support or promote specific events, promotions or special offers.)
11. Facebook Ad campaigns (see Adwords.)
12. Blog (written, video and/or audio)
13. Articles on article sites, like ehow.com, ezinearticles.com, articlebase.com, etc.
14. Post on community sites such as Digg and Squidoo.
15. Answer questions on Yahoo Answers
16. Auto responders

Printed Materials:
17. Posters
18. Leaflets
19. Lead boxes, (special cardboard or plastic boxes, into which people can drop their details, that are left at carefully selected locations.)
20. Post cards
21. Door hangers (like those in hotels)
22. Welcome packs
23. Stationery
24. T-shirts
25. Hoodies
26. Baseball caps and beanies
27. Car door magnets
28. Windscreen stickers (decals)
29. Training handbooks for students
30. Newspaper ads
31. Banners, flags, A-boards
32. Promotional materials (pens, key-rings, mouse mats, water bottles, etc.)

External events:

33. Demos
34. School assembly talks
35. High Street Canvassing
36. Crashing events, i.e. making yourself visible by wearing t-shirts and/or hats at fairs, exhibitions, processions, etc.
37. Street parties
38. Charity events like board breaking or Sparathons
39. Mall booths , i.e. hiring space for a stall at your local shopping centre.
40. Business promotions

The key thing to remember here is that you should always have several activities going on at the same time to keep the flow of enquiries going. Relying on only one of these is a bit like sitting on a one legged chair, once it goes you become invisible to anyone looking for your services and potential students will flock to whoever is (more) visible than you. Even a website doesn't guarantee you consistent exposure as Google and other search engines constantly adapt their search criteria.

As a rule of thumb have at least five or six things going at the same time, the more the better. The key is to be consistent. There's no point in only sticking posters up once a year; people can sometimes take a lot of time to finally get started and a consistent poster presence reassures the public that you are here to stay.

Internal marketing activities are aimed at getting your students to refer and recommend you to friends, colleagues and family members. It crosses over into customer care.

These can involve:

41. Prize draws and social events
42. Pizza parties
43. Movie nights

44. Sleep-overs for kids
45. Paintball days out for your adult members
46. Internal tournaments
47. Seminars for newcomers and friends of students
48. Summer Camps
49. Guest instructor workshops (perhaps invite your teacher(s))
50. Raffles and price draw competitions for referrals
51. Newsletters
52. Postcards for birthdays, graduations, sickness
53. Reward badges
54. Surveys
55. 'Well Done' calls
56. Student of the Month awards
57. Additional classes, like fitness, sparring, weapons, forms, clinic, etc.

Unlike external marketing, many of these are often aimed to coincide with public holidays or celebrations such as Valentines, Mothers Day, Fathers Day, Halloween, Christmas, etc. If you regularly frequent a supermarket you will have noticed the (very predictable) promotions that chase each other every year. As soon as Halloween has come and gone, you start to see early Christmas promotions.

These continual promotions are repeated over and over again because they work. All you have to do is to copy what works.

Internal Referrals are the cheapest and most powerful tool to grow your school. Don't let any of your students off the hook until they have referred someone; keep asking them to invite someone else to their training until they have done so. More about how you can increase referrals a little later.

As you can see, it is quite a job to stay focused and on top of all of this, which is why it's so important to have your marketing events planned and prepared way in advance. Which leads us nicely to your marketing plan.

*"Strategy and timing are the Himalayas of marketing.
Everything else is the Catskills."*

AL RIES

The good news is that many of these marketing opportunities are tied to annual events and seasons. That makes them predictable, so to take full advantage you just need to time your efforts correctly. Armed with my marketing diary, I prefer to plan my monthly marketing activities at least a month in advance. This helps me to budget for it, which has the further advantage that I am not so easily lured off course. Thinking back to my first couple of years in business I've certainly been there and done that. There is a big difference between a *good idea* and a viable marketing strategy that will actually produce some return on investment. Family members are particularly unhelpful when it comes to deciding where to spend money on advertising, unless they either have hands-on business acumen or are offering to pay for it out of their own pocket. Both scenarios are usually unlikely and for good reason.

Remember to keep a record in your marketing diary of how it went and what kind of response you received, which can be best measured by the quantity and quality of leads and sign-ups you managed to generate from that the event or campaign.

Plan your work and then work the plan. Don't get side-tracked by "good ideas" and "special offers".

So what's the best way of putting together an effective marketing plan for your school?

Well, here's more good news, you can find a complete annual marketing plan template on the KickStart website. You can either just copy and implement it or use it as a template for your own plan. As long as you are disciplined and consistent with it you should see a pretty steady flow of new students every month.

FROM LEAD GENERATION TO LEAD MANAGEMENT

In a sales environment new customers are nurtured and developed via a process called a "pipeline". The pipeline starts with so-called suspects, and progresses through prospects, leads and ends in sales – or enrolments/sign-ups as we prefer to call them. Everybody who hasn't (yet) expressed an interest in your classes and services, but is physically and financially able to do so is considered a "suspect", these obviously rank quite low in your sales pipeline. Once somebody has expressed such an interest by calling, emailing or personal contact is officially considered a (cold) lead or a prospect. Now it is your job to develop prospects into hot leads. Hot leads are prospects, who have made some effort to find out about you and perhaps even booked an induction session with you. If they actually turn up then they become potential sign-ups. If they don't become members of your prestigious establishment, they are on their way to becoming cold leads again if you don't look after them. A good way to keep reminding them that you are still there is put them on your mailing list or auto-responder list. This process of keeping your pipeline of new students continuously filled and flowing is called lead management. It is crucial that you understand and master it.

THE KICKSTART PROGRESS CHART (KPC)

A vital tool in helping you to stay on top of your lead generation / lead management efforts is the KickStart Progress Chart (KPC), which is a tracking worksheet. As you can only control what you can measure, numbers are your new best friends. You will be amazed what a difference this little sheet of paper can make in your marketing efforts!

The KPC will help you to stay on track, as it will highlight any areas that you are not doing, or upon which you could be improving, to maximise the effectiveness of your marketing efforts. Together with a friend or a coach you will also set in place the accountability to help you succeed. A KPC worksheet is best kept on a weekly basis and should list all your daily and weekly marketing activities and successes.

I have partially completed a sample KPC for you. Each column represents a single working day for which you need to make the following daily entries:

Mood Barometer

On a scale of 1-10, ten being the highest, how much does your daily mind set and how you feel physically, influence you performance? This score is highly revealing as it will tell you how your physical and mental state will impact on your marketing performance. This might be a bit more intuitive in nature but is, none the less, well worth measuring.

Project Barometer

This score will let you keep your finger on the pulse of how you are getting on with specific projects and tasks, such as event planning, writing projects, learning goals, etc. Most of us are good starters but poor finishers. There is no substitute for persistence, especially once we encounter the first signs of defeat.

This is measured by percentage of completion until a score of 100% is attained, which means it is done.

Daily / Weekly Actions

As mentioned before, if you are to make your marketing work for you, you need to have several things going on at any one time. These can include internal as well as external marketing actions. There is a simple yes (Y) or no (N) answer for each activity. All completed activities or actions are then added up at the bottom to give you a total score. There should be a balance of daily and weekly actions.

If you haven't followed through on a weekly activity you must give yourself a negative (N) score for that, at the end of the week. As these scores are for you alone there is really no point in cheating.

Target Scores

You need to be clear about where your activities are supposed to get you, such as how many leads, inductions and enrolments you actually need. Break down bigger goals into smaller manageable tasks. Be exact and calculate your hit-rate in percentage terms. This score is likely to go up as you become better and more effective.

Favourite Excuse

We are all experts in coming up with reasons why we can't do something. It is called creating avoidance. We all do it and the only way to get on top of it, is to firstly be consciously aware of the fact that we are doing it. Record your favourite excuse for not following through with any of your marketing activities as you planned and then indicate via a yes (Y) or no (N) score which one got to you the most. Self mastery is the hardest job you will ever tackle. Conquering the enemy within is one of the highest achievements of martial arts training. If you don't, it will get the better of you. By stepping in front of the mirror you will see that your inner self is both your best friend and at the same time your worst enemy. Powerful stuff!

You can download a worksheet template from the KickStart website www.martialartsbusinessschool.com

KICK START PROGRESS CHART									
Mood Barometer (1-10 scale)									
Physical	9	8	5	7	9				
Mental	7	7	6	8	7				
Project Barometer (% done)									
Organised Summer Camp	10	10	0	15	0				
Reading Talib's book	10	25	50	70	100				
Found school for assembly talk	0	0	0	33	33				
Daily/Weekly Activities (Y/N)									
1) Putting up posters	N	Y	Y	N	Y				
2) Servicing Leadboxes / wk	Y	N	N	N	Y				
3) Canvasing	Y	Y	Y	Y	Y				
4) Asked for referal	Y	Y	N	Y	N				
5) Call backs	Y	Y	Y	N	Y				
6) Blogged on website / wk	Y	N	N	N	N				
7) Door to door leaflets	N	N	Y	N	Y				
8) Updated Newsletter	N	N	N	N	Y				
9) Facebook / Google Ads / wk	Y	N	N	N	N				
10) Public demo / wk	N	Y	N	N	Y				
Total (# out of 10)	6	5	4	2	7				
Targets (% of target)									
6 Leads	100	0	50	70	100				
4 Inductions	70	30	50	100	0				
1 Enrolment	0	100	0	100	100				
Favourite Excuse									
Designing new leaflet	N	N	N	N	Y				
Busy training	N	Y	Y	N	N				
Too tired	Y	N	N	Y	N				

Start Date:

Name:

THE STUDENT LIFE CYCLE

Now that you understand what a lead is and how to manage it, let's look at the life cycle of everybody that moves through your school. There is a basic four-stage process, which is very well understood in marketing, that every one of your students goes through. It is called AIDA, which stands for:

Attention (or Awareness)
Potential students need to know that you exist in the first place before anything else can happen. This is the job of, for example, your advertising, blog, social media post or sponsorship. It needs to grab their attention and generate excitement. Giving away free stuff like tips and advice can be very effective in generating awareness and in building trust. The same is true for special offers and discounts.

Interest

Now that you have their attention you need to create an interest by telling them how your classes can enhance their lives. Make sure to talk about benefits not features, i.e. there's no point in saying that your style is the best or that you can break concrete with your head. Explain why it is the best from a new learner's perspective, e.g. it can make you fit and teach you how to defend yourself at the same time. Answer "How" questions instead of "What" questions.

Desire

Now make them really want it! Do this with time-bound offers, money-back guarantees or bonuses for bringing a friend.

Action

This is the step that's most often forgotten. You need to tell your potential students and/or parents what to do! Examples include "CALL NOW TO BOOK YOUR FREE TRIAL SESSION" and "Win 30 days FREE Martial Arts Training!"

When designing marketing material, which includes your website, run it through the A.I.D.A. formula to make sure it has the greatest impact and the best chance of success.

This is however a linear approach and not a cycle as the existing student continues to play an important role in the marketing of your school. Back in 2008, Dave Evans came up with a new way by incorporating the increasingly important social media into the customer life cycle. If we combine this with the marketing AIDA model, we arrive at a full circle of enrolling and referring that breaks away from the traditional linear AIDA model.

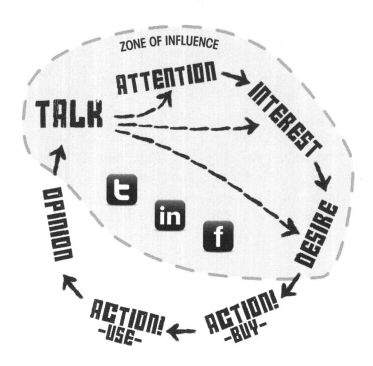

Use

Once you have gained a new student, he/she will (hopefully) use your service. This might be a one-off class or may extend for months or years.

Opinion

As your student(s) continue to use your services, they will develop an opinion as to whether it meets their expectations established in the interest phase and whether the value proposition was correct. So it is important that you only promise what you can deliver and do not create false expectations. Under-promising and over-delivering works wonders here.

Talk

Once your students have started to use your classes they should be encouraged to give online feedback and share their opinion of your school. This should be done immediately post sale by a timely email requesting the new student to leave a comment for others on your website or on Google reviews. After your student has obliged by giving you a raving review you should ask them to share the review with their network of contacts via social media (via Facebook, Twitter, YouTube, etc.).

Importantly, the above user-generated comments and testimonials should help in attracting future students' attention, interest and desire, keeping your sales pipeline fuelled. This occurs in the "zone of influence".

Generating informal/unsolicited feedback is more difficult, where the student posts comments or videos directly to their social networks. You need to monitor these networks so that you react to negative feedback and promote positive feedback.

Special Tip

A great way to keep tabs on who is saying what about you online, is to use the free Google Alerts service. All you need is a free Google account to set it up. Google Alerts is also an effective way to keep up to date on your competition or with any developments or news in your chosen style.

Conversion Rates

All the leads in the world mean very little if you can't look after and convert your leads to sign-ups. Your success as an instructor and school owner largely depend on how good you are in dazzling browsers with your wit and expertise, so that they bite off your hand.

The rate at which you convert potential students into actual paying members is largely determined by

- The quality of the lead
- The consistency of the follow up
- Your presentation and/or communication skills

I work on a conversation rate of 5-3-1, that means that for every new member that turns up and joins I need at least three people who have booked an induction session. To get to three appointments experience has taught me that I need at least five names and numbers, which we get via various marketing activities, like online enquiries, walk-bys, calls from posters or details we collect during various events. Your conversion rate might initially be a bit lower, i.e. you probably need more cold leads to get to an enrolment, as you need to become better at getting people to commit to you by making a payment.

This formula will help you to set yourself realistic and achievable targets. For example, if you want to get your school to 100 students in let's say six months you need to recruit four new students per week. That means that you need to have twelve appointments booked, which you get from twenty cold leads per week. If you work six days per week that means that all you have to do is to get three names and numbers per day. If you have anything from 6-10 different marketing tools in play at any given time this shouldn't be that hard to achieve. Once you are set-up it is all a question of planning your marketing and then just working the plan in a disciplined and consistent manner without too much second guessing. If you are ambitious you can turn beating your targets into a game and keep setting yourself higher targets. Use the KickStart Progress Chart to track your performance and repeat this mantra daily: "If it is to be, it is up to me".

Meet The Teflon Man

In order to keep yourself motivated you need to make yourself rejection proof. You can't be everything to everybody and many will turn you down. If a prospect says "No" all it really means is that you either haven't given them enough reasons to buy from you or that they are simply not in the market for your services, at least not for now.

Many of my students have told me that they had been thinking about doing some martial art for years before they finally got around to start training. This is to illustrate that, although many will tell you that they won't join your school when asked, it only means that it isn't right for them at the moment. "No" really ever means "not now" and is not to be confused with a total rejection of either you or your school. Don't take rejection personal, it isn't unless you make it so.

> "I take rejection as someone blowing a bugle in my ear to wake me up and get me going, rather than retreat."
> **SYLVESTER STALLONE**

It is your job to stay in touch with them until they either tell you in no uncertain terms that they would rather chew on rusty razor blades than join your school or their personal circumstances have changed and they are ready to enrol. As long as you do it in a polite and professional way it's not stalking or harassment and the prospect can always opt out. If someone is not interested that's OK, simply move on to the next prospect.

Remember: Some will, some won't. So what! Who's next?

THE NEW RULES OF MARTIAL ARTS MARKETING (INTERNET AND SOCIAL MEDIA)

> "Guerrilla marketing requires that you be very technocozy; if you're not, your technophobia is holding back your small business. If you suffer from that affliction, make an appointment with your technoshrink immediately. Technophobia is fatal these days."
> **JAY C. LEVINSON**

Like it or not the internet is the game changer. Nothing compares to the way you can reach an audience currently via the World Wide Web. It is the most powerful marketing tool that you currently have at your disposal and gives you an unfair advantage over much bigger competitors. It enables you to do what companies with big budgets can do without the big budget. Your future students and/or their parents expect to find you online at will 24/7, 365 days of the year. They have the attention span of a house fly and are spoiled rotten by thousands of cool and captivating websites vying for their attention and their disposable income.

All these mind boggling high tech possibilities for gaining and retaining students do of course bear their own pitfalls. The one thing to keep in mind about the internet is that it is forever changing and evolving. Twelve months is a long time when it comes to the web and once-popular websites can fall almost into obscurity over that period. Marketing strategies that would have given you at least a half decent return on investment six months ago might no longer work. Just look at sites like Facebook or Twitter which are frequently changing, not just in appearance. Your internet marketing needs to take this constant evolution into account if you want prospective students to take you seriously and to take the next step once they have found you.

If your website isn't part of the solution it may well become part of the problem. I predict that in little more than five years the web will be the only way in which people will look for anything from martial arts tuition to matrimonial services, mostly from their ever more sophisticated mobile devices.

DID YOU KNOW?
To date almost half of UK internet users are going
online via mobile phone data connections, according to
the Office for National Statistics.

As a full-time "marketeer" I make it my business to keep my finger on the fast changing pulse of the internet to make sure that my website does what it is supposed to – generate new enquiries.

In today's interconnected world, where everything seems accessible at your fingertips, it is absolutely vital to have a web presence that is well thought through and deliberate. It needs to fulfil the following three criteria:

- It must reflect the professional image of you and your school.
- It has to prompt people to take action (pick up the phone or shoot you an email) and
- Rank at the top of Google for your area.

If it lacks one or the other it only helps your competition to look good and will in fact cost you business and credibility. But that's just half the story; according to Facebook there are there are now over 950 million (and counting) active users on Facebook worldwide! All major companies, actors, politicians and institutions have a fan page on Facebook. If you still think that it is only for geeks and bored students than you need to wake up and smell the coffee.

Internet marketing for the savvy martial arts school owner means that you have to proactively get eyeballs on your site and, much more than that, get them to take action.

Your website not only needs to be easily found, easy to use, fast to load (especially on mobile devices) but, above all has to guide your visitors to take the next step in becoming members of your school. Just take a look around websites that offer martial arts classes in your town or city. The majority are utterly clueless when it comes to using the web to their advantage. Here are some instant turn-offs when it comes to people visiting your internet presence:

Doesn't Look The Part
Your site may be visually overloaded with pictures and blinking icons and generally creates the impression that it was patched together by

a school boy in his bedroom over the weekend. This looks unprofessional and tells the visitor that you are a hobbyist at best. Use a free Wordpress template (Google if unsure) and keep your site clean with professional-looking pictures. You can get great looking pics on sites like flikr.com or via Google search. If you don't mind paying a little there are several so called royalty free sites, like istockphotos.com, gettyimages.co.uk or martialartsgraphics.net that allow you to download quality images for a small fee. Please make sure not to violate any copyrights, as this is a headache you don't need.

Out Of Date

Visitors will leave your site in seconds if the contents are obviously out of date and the site was last updated perhaps twelve months ago or longer. This tells the visitor that if you care that much about your first impressions, you are likely to care just as much about your clients and students. This is also a complete turn off if you want Google to list your site towards the top of your local search results. Get a blog going and post stuff like news and videos at least every week, or get someone to do it for you. It's free and gives visitors a reason to return.

Fresh **Content Is King!**

The best website isn't going to help you without good and up-to-date content. Most visitors to your website are no longer prepared to spend time reading poorly written copy; people expect video for at least some of the content on your site.

Here are some shocking facts from one of the most popular video sites online, YouTube:

- Forty-eight hours of video are uploaded every minute, resulting in nearly eight years of content uploaded every day.
- Over three billion videos are viewed a day and users upload the equivalent of 240,000 full-length films every week.

- More video is uploaded to YouTube in one month than the three major US networks created in sixty years.
- YouTube's demographic is broad: 18-54 years old
- YouTube reached over 700 billion playbacks in 2010
- 800 million unique users visit YouTube each month

And that's just YouTube; there are of course many other video sharing sites online, including blib.tv, vimeo.com, viddler.com, and dailymotion.com amongst others. I think you get the idea here.

Self Glorification

There are still plenty of websites for martial arts schools that like to be either some kind of Wikipedia for their respective style, or worse, are all about the instructor. They like to dazzle with how many belts or tournaments he has won or how many boards his eminence the supreme grand master can break with his little pinky.

Another instant turn-off for many, especially parents, is the depiction of sometimes graphic violence or the endorsement and glorification of violence or violent behaviour. Not only do most people not really care how tough (someone might think) they are, many would feel uncomfortable with pandering to some inflated ego – and people wonder why there are so few women practicing martial arts.

Remember to highlight benefits not features. Everybody's favourite radio station is and always has been WI-FM, which stands for "What's In it For Me". That is to say that people are predominantly interested in what something or someone can do for them. Ranting on about some style or master says nothing about how it can help and benefit a new comer to your school. All that chest-beating might do is attract all the wrong kinds of people.

Out Of Touch

One of the things I often hear from people who come to either check out our school, or after they have enrolled with us, is that they have contacted other schools via their website or even left a voice message but never received a reply (I sometimes like to thank my competitors for making my job easy at times). You might as well not have a website if it is neither easy nor obvious how to get in touch, but this is compounded if nobody replies or replies late to new enquiries. It's like having a shop without a door; an annoying waste of space. Make sure your contact details are up-to-date and easy to find on every page of your site. Go back and test that the details and forms you provide on your site still work and that you get any and all enquiries forwarded onto your mobile device. And don't forget to spell check every page thoroughly!

At our school we use a professional answer service for less than £100 per month that not only ensures all enquiries are handled in a prompt and professional manner, it also filters all those time wasters who want to sell you double glazed windows over the phone.

TOOLS OF THE TRADE

"Never let your ads write Cheques that your website can't cash."
AVINASH KAUSHIK

When it comes to marketing and advertising your school or club you cannot rely on a single track approach. As much as you need a very thought-through online presence you can't rely on it alone. Many of the more conventional or old style ways to promote your services are still very effective if only to drive traffic to your site, which is the next stop for many if they want to check you out. In your continuous search for new students you need to realise that martial arts marketing is a two way street. People can either search you out or get referred to you by others or you need to alert them to the fact that you exist and to the benefits of your training to them. Remember to focus on benefits not features.

Your extensive equipment, big hall, or years of teaching experience are all great features, but they do not tell the potential student what you can do for them. To understand this better make a list of all the things that you can offer a potential, new and/or existing student and next to it list in what way this will help them. Ask "how" questions instead of "what" questions. Once you have established what your strengths are you need to make sure that these feature on all your promotional material in a consistent way. Find your niche and do not try to be everything to everybody.

Here are some tried and tested ways, in detail, that will help to promote your school at minimum cost:

Posters

Still an old favourite, albeit being definitely a passive tool, they will serve in creating awareness for your school and help in marking your territory. As I mentioned before, resist the temptation to use any imagery that could be seen as being violent or portray martial arts as a blood sport. Silhouetted pictures and a snappy headline are effective in catching the eye and in getting the onlooker to read further. Ensure every week that your posters are up and not ripped or drawn on. You can get some great deals on posters online. Check out: www.printcarrier.com or fairprint.co.uk.

Flyers And Postcards

As with posters, I would suggest you get everything printed to a single design to ensure that you display a unified and professional image. Folded flyers are a nice touch for walk-bys – people who just drop by unannounced to check out times and prices. Avoid scribbling details down on scraps of paper, as this does your image no good. Imagine what that person will take into closer consideration once he/she has scoped several schools to then make an educated decision about going along for a trial session. The same logos and message should also be on any postcards you are planning to hand out in the town centre. A very effective trick to stop people binning your promotional material is to give it some value. I use the rear side of my postcards to print useful self-defence tips. Although they might not consider that a martial arts or self-defence class is the right thing at this moment, they might well keep the card for the neat tips on the back and stick it to their fridge. You can also offer to print promotional flyers for a local travel agency, that include your travel safety tips with all your details on. If you need some affordable designs you might like to check out websites such as www.fiverr.com where you can get people to do your design work for five dollars. If you want faster or higher quality you can always negotiate some favourable deals.

Lead Boxes

Another great way of generating cheap leads to keep your enquiry pipeline full, is the use of so called lead boxes.

These are made from cardboard or plastic and can be placed in shops, restaurants, hairdressers, takeaways, post offices or anywhere else where people have to wait to get served. They typically have little pads with enquiry forms, and have a pen attached, which allows people to leave their details by entering some kind of competition for example.

But don't just drop them off somewhere. Meet the manager of the business and offer him/her an exchange for trialling your boxes in their establishment. Only leave your boxes in a place if they continue to generate leads and service them weekly. Replace or restock them if they are damaged or the pads or pens are gone and re-home them quickly if they don't yield you any leads. Lead boxes are a bit more of an investment and are fairly high maintenance, so, as with all your consistent marketing efforts, you need to be focused and disciplined. You can get lead boxes from places like leadbox.com or www.future-fitness.com. I had to order mine from the U.S.A.

Car Advertisement

If you are into low cost advertising you have to make good use of what you already have. If you have a car, use it as a free medium on which to advertise your school. Also get your students to advertise your school on their cars in return for free training or equipment. For very little money you can get customised magnetic car signs that go on car doors. Or, for a little more permanent fixtures use removable car window stickers displaying your website address. I have used www.vistaprint.co.uk for car door magnets and window decal stickers. You can of course use lead boxes to hang off your car windows when you are parked for shopping.

Printed Advertisement

I think that it's a bit like the Marmite of marketing, as it tends to work for some but not for others. My personal experiences with putting printed ads in newspapers and magazines are not good. They cost a lot of money and appear only once. In my humble view these offer only a very modest return on investment. You might be much better off using that money on more targeted advertising, such as Facebook or Google. The advantage is that you can chop, change and stop your ads daily if they don't get you any results.

Social Media

As mentioned previously, they offer much greater flexibility when compared to printed ads. Facebook in particular offers extremely targeted advertising, which you can customise to age, gender, city or catchment area or to people who have expressed interest in specific activities. If nothing else they will generate a bit of traffic to your website which also helps with your Google ranking. The reason I'm mainly referring to Google when I talk about internet search engines is because they have over 90% of the market share in the UK. In other words, I wouldn't waste much time and effort on other search engines like Bing or Yahoo, unless you are not in the UK of course.

A much underused resource for getting your website ranked high in Google or Yahoo (also called Search Engine Optimisation or SEO) and to get people interested in what you have to offer is YouTube. You can create your own YouTube Channel for free and post regular short videos on there. All you need to do is to set-up a free YouTube account. As YouTube is now owned by Google, it means that you need to get a free Gmail account. If you already have one, you can use it to create your YouTube account.

Here are some tips to make your YouTube videos more effective.
- Don't try to sell anything. Keep your clips short, informative and if possible entertaining. Avoid turning them into an ad.

- Make your videos viral. Post them on as many websites (as well as other video hosting sites) as possible. You can also outsource that via fiverr.com. Make sure to link them on your Facebook, Twitter and LinkedIn pages.
- If you are not using a professional editing service or software don't worry too much about perfection. However try to get as much resolution as possible and ensure that the sound is as clear as you can get it. I bought a small but very effective little camera for my podcasts and YouTube videos that does the trick. It's not much bigger than a mobile phone and records in HD. It's a Kodak Zi8 and costs less than £80 on eBay. You can read some reviews here: http://amzn.to/Inlj3X.

Brand it. Make sure to keep a consistent format to your videos. Use a specific intro and music that makes it your brand. This includes using your logo and website address, which should appear at the beginning and end of the clip.

Retake. Make several dry runs and rehearse your material without making the end product look rehearsed or like a performance. Be yourself and use clear and simple language. Retake as much as you like until you feel comfortable. Remember that nothing online is really perfect and of professional quality, unless of course you have a big studio backing you.

Tell a Story. Everybody loves a good story, but don't just stand there and talk. Try to make it exiting and entertaining without venturing into Jackass territory. If you can, storyboard your clip to keep it short, sharp and to the point. YouTube videos are typically no longer than ten minutes in length. Try to make people want to see the next part by breaking a subject matter into several parts.

Get Comments. Ask your viewers to leave a comment and delete all negative ones.

Look and learn. If you are still a bit unsure look at what others are doing and just copy a style that you like and that get a lot of views. Above all, enjoy yourself and have fun with it, without getting carried away. Avoid using coarse language and/or cuss words.

Referrals

One of the cheapest and most important sources for growing your school are referrals from existing students. But in order for people to refer you to their friends and family you need to give them something to talk about. The best way to become highly referable is to under-promise and over-deliver. You must regularly and often go out of your way to impress your students and I don't mean by showing off. Why? Because people have been sold, scammed, played and screwed with and they are tired of it. Every ad promises something it most likely can't keep, like a man being chased by female admirers because he used a particular anti-perspirant spray; and we know it!

Here are five things that will help you to become more referable to your students:

1. **Passion!** Nothing comes even close to an unbridled passion for a subject. It is highly infectious and second to none in creating a buzz in your school. You will always hear about someone who has his/her whole heart invested in their subject matter.

2. **Become *the* expert in your field.** Everybody wants to train with the top expert in any chosen field of expertise. Make sure that you keep yourself well informed about what's going on in the world of martial arts so you can give informed and

insightful views on things. Become a source of inspiration and don't be bashful. Make sure people know that you are the genuine article. Nothing quite works like becoming a published author in your field to make you an authority.

3. **Be Reliable.** Answer every email, pick up the phone when it rings, be on time for classes and with product orders and your refer-ability will sky rocket. People normally hate change and nothing undermines your credibility more than chopping and changing what you do.

4. **Ask for it!** This might seem pretty obvious, but you would be surprised how many instructors assume that if they did all the above that their students would talk about nothing but them. Don't be afraid to ask your students for help in growing your school. Most people who feel that they are part of something greater than themselves love to help spread the word especially if the person they admire and respect (that's you) asks them for help.

5. **Incentivise**. Few things work better in getting people to act on your behalf than an ethical bribe. Give students something in return for every single person they bring into your school. This could be a cash prize, a free upgrade to a higher programme or perhaps some private training. Most importantly, thank and praise them in front of others to keep them happy and motivated.

RAPID RECAP – ATTRACTING STUDENTS

- Students (both new and loyal regulars) are the lifeblood of any martial arts business.
- Marketing is way too important to leave to somebody else – you need to take responsibility, make important decisions and get expert help to produce materials that work.
- Quality and quantity are not mutually exclusive. You want to be able to turn people away because your classes are oversubscribed.
- Remember the three Rs of marketing – Recruitment, Retention, Recall.
- Set yourself ambitious goals and then ask yourself how to get there. How soon can you get to 100 students?
- Marketing is not the same as PR but equally important.
- Always keep a good balance of internal and external marketing. Plan it in advance and make sure to have several things working for you at any one time.

SHOW ME THE MONEY!

*"The surest way to ruin a man who does not know
how to handle money is to give him some."*
GEORGE BERNARD SHAW

If you want to succeed in running your own MA school, or club, either full-time or part-time, you need to know about financial management. It doesn't matter how many black belts you have or how many tournaments you have won. It doesn't even matter if you are a great instructor and even fantastic at promoting yourself. The money you earn will slip between your fingers if you don't know how to efficiently collect it, keep track of it, save it, and spend or invest it wisely.

Poor financial management is one of the leading reasons that martial arts schools fail. In many cases, failure could have been avoided if the owners had applied sound financial principles to all their dealings and decisions. Financial management is not something that you can leave to your banker, financial planner, or accountant — you need to understand the basic principles yourself and use them on a daily basis, even if you plan to leave the more complicated work to hired professionals.

Financial management includes the following areas:
- **Your basic bookkeeping** – this involves the daily recording of any earnings, any work with your accountant and understanding financial statements.
- **Credit and collections** – this includes deciding how to charge, if you should accept any card payments and how to make sure that you effectively collect all the money owed to you by your students.
- **Managing your cash flow** – describes the way money flows in

and out of your hands and how to reduce the lag between cash-outflows and cash inflows.
- **Major purchases and projects** – shows you how to calculate larger investments in capital equipment and business facilities.
- **Analysing your current financial position** – this delves a little more into sophisticated ways to look into your financial statements and other aspects of your business to identify trends, spot problems and to see how you compare to other schools throughout the country.

We will mainly be dealing with the first three aspects as they relate more to the set-up of your school or club. Following volumes of this guide will get into the other aspects a bit more as your school grows and matures.

PRICING STRATEGIES

The correct pricing policy is a critical success factor for your school. Adopting a more strategic approach to pricing can have a major impact on the trajectory of the entire business.

When it comes to charging your members it is important that you have a clear pricing policy in place and understand why, how much and how to charge your students.

Many instructors and school owners I know believe that potential and existing students prioritise price ahead of quality or service. I haven't come across any compelling evidence to support this and would advise you to be very reluctant to promote price as your key differentiator.

In his audio book "How to sell higher priced products against lower priced competition", famous business author Brian Tracy reveals that a recent Harvard Study discovered that in fact only 6% of all sales are determined by price alone.

How To Choose Your Price

Your customers will quickly provide you with feedback on whether you have chosen the right price for your services. If it's too high, you will lose the student, set it too low and you leave money on the table. So, in choosing the right price for the classes in our school what factors should we consider?

The following are practical tips that are based both upon what I have seen work spectacularly well and upon things that have caused truly disastrous consequences. "How will I know which is which?" you might ask. Don't worry, you will.

1. **No Surprises.** Always make sure that your potential student and/or their parent(s) understands and agrees in advance how much it is and what other costs are involved, like equipment, seminars, gradings. Nasty surprises cause instant dissatisfaction and any compromises result in both parties losing out.

2. **Use price as a tool to customise demand** and thereby choose the kind of students you want to win, retain and lose. It seems an obvious and rather a general rule, but for most products and services increasing price tends to lower demand and reducing price should increase it. However, as a premier provider you don't want to attract everyone. So, I recommend to increase the price just enough to attract, what I call 'B' grade students, but deter 'C's. 'C's typically create too much effort when compared to the reward, eat into profits and take the focus away from the valuable 'A's and 'B's. Remember the Pareto (80:20) rule?
   20% of your students generate 80% of your sales.
   20% of your students produce 80% of your profits.
   20% of your students/parents cause 80% of your hassle.

3. **No discount without reducing something** in the value proposition, unless you are planning to do a time-bound promotion. Controversial? Think about it this way: Most people subconsciously align the perceived value of what you are offering with the attached cost. Hence the expression "You get what you pay for".

4. **Arrive at your price from two angles**:
   a) The traditional 'cost plus' calculation, i.e. labour, overheads plus a little profit for you of course and
   b) What the market is likely to pay for your classes, based on the prices your competitors charge. Market research is essential here, which will give you much needed certainty on how to position your services. You would be surprised how many martial arts schools don't bother to do this.

5. **Believe!** Once you have completed your market research and carefully selected your pricing structure you must have the courage to believe in it. Don't apologise, justify or feel embarrassed by it. I gained a different perspective on my monthly rate when I found out that a solicitor I used to write a letter for me, charges £200 for the privilege. Remember what I said about the perception issue above.

6. **Is it in demand?** Check where your classes are on their life-cycle. If it is something that is really in demand, like MMA or perhaps some military combat system, it should produce plenty of interest and students and the price is less important to the buyer. If what you teach is in decline or available everywhere for next to nothing, then demand might be shrinking. Awareness and knowledge will help you to make your pricing decisions obvious.

7. **Don't be a copy-cat.** Look for innovative ways to set your offering apart through your pricing policy. You certainly don't want to enter price wars by trying to be the cheapest. Explore other ideas. Can you fix or guarantee your price in some way? How about linking your price to a specific value?

8. **Don't make price the issue.** People don't look for "the cheapest" price; they more often want the best price based on quality, availability and service. You might get more traction from a "fixed-price", "flexible", "value based" or even "most expensive". We will talk more about price buyers later.

Special Tip:
If you have any hang ups, or hesitate when it comes to asking for the money, you will appear insincere and even dodgy. Role play how to ask for money and get your friends to come up with objections and questions.

Being Reassuringly Expensive
Earlier I went on about confidence and self believe. This is where it comes to show. When I first started teaching, I was confident enough to take on a couple of street thugs (at least I thought I was) but when it came to ask someone for a £99 enrolment fee, I was ringing my clam hands and felt very uncomfortable. Thinking back I must have looked really insincere, but people still paid it. Today this is no longer an issue for me or my instructors under me and I frequently ask for and receive thousands of pounds in tuition fees up front. It's only ever an issue if you make it one. As long as your students can see the value of what you are offering it's great for all involved. Your students will be more committed to you and your school and (could) have saved a lot of money. In turn you should have more disposable income to keep your doors open.

Here are seven solid reasons why you should charge as much money as possible for your classes.

- **Bigger margins.** Ultimately we are in business to make a profit. Because the cost of supplying your classes remains relatively constant, the higher the prices the higher the profit, the higher the profit, the more money ends up in your personal bank account, on your driveway or in your home (or in my wife's case, in her wardrobe!).

- **Less is more**. When you charge premium prices and make larger profits, you can afford to work with a smaller number or a more selective group of students, meaning less hassle, less organisation and crucially you can be far more selective about who you accept into your school. Believe me, you don't want to be in a position where you have to accept just anybody who walks through your doors.

- **Better Students**. By becoming the premium martial arts school in your area, you automatically eliminate the time wasters. You'll only ever see serious students who, incidentally, are infinitely more committed to working with you, meaning fewer cancellations, rescheduling, refunds, etc.

- **Better results.** When people pay top rate for a service, they want to make the most of it. Premium clients/students are far more likely to actually turn up to classes, come to seminars and gradings and are more dedicated to reaching their black belt. Therefore the results your students will get will be considerably better than anyone else in your market place. Thus, justifying your prices and becoming a positively reinforcing, upwards spiral, of higher prices and better results.

- **No price wars.** Because you aren't competing on price, you cannot be undercut by the competition. This concept may be difficult for some to grasp until they've tried it, but it will be even more difficult for your competitors to grasp when they cut their prices, and all their students are still flocking to you!

- **Less competition.** Ferrari doesn't have to compete with Ford, Vauxhall, Skoda, etc, they (the 94% of non-Ferrari sellers) can fight it out amongst themselves for the low price, low profit end of the market. Just like Apple computers or Gucci handbags, Ferrari hold a unique position in the market place meaning, when customers come to them, price is not an issue. Who would you rather be: Ferrari, or Skoda? Gucci or the local charity shop?
- **Economic peril.** Whilst at the time of writing, we are right in the middle of a double dip recession and the economic recovery is dragging on, things are getting tighter and tighter for average families of average means. Do you really want to be fighting it out for sales from people with no money? Or would you rather be dealing with people of much greater financial means, who are far less affected by the current economic climate because they have a much larger disposable income?

Raising my prices has had a dramatic impact on our student numbers. When I finally got over my defeatist self-talk and doubled my prices from £49 to £99 per month my student count doubled within six months.

I had previously struggled like mad for almost five years to get beyond fifty students and no matter what I tried, I couldn't do it. Not only did I double my prices I also shortened my class duration for beginners. And people loved it! There are, of course a few people who did not like what they heard, especially those who had done martial arts before and were used to ninety minute classes and pay-as-you-go, but these were not the kind of students I was after anymore. In short there is really only one way to make more money and that is to ask for it.

Special Tip:
Keep the existing members on the price they are used to and apply the increase only to the newcomers as they don't know any different. If anyone should ever challenge you on this you can point out that the old price was simply an introductory offer which no longer applies. Asking existing students for more money without a perceived increase in what they get in return is a sure fire way to cull or even kill your student count.

DECIDING HOW TO CHARGE

Before you open your doors to the public, it is essential that you not only have a clear pricing policy but also decide how you are going to collect your money. When I first started teaching back in the early nineties I charged £3.50 on the door, I later put my prices up to £5 per session. That was nearly twenty years ago! Back then I was teaching for the love of it and to finance my own training, which is obviously a very different motivation to running your own full-time academy.

I'm not saying that you won't have any students if you offer pay-as-you-go (PAYG) but I would seriously consider the downsides to that. With a view to your future wouldn't you ideally like to build something that has some staying power even if you might not be personally around to teach every single class?

PAYG is, in my view, the worst kind of option from an instructors point of view and it also tends to sabotage the students in the long run. Here are five good reasons why you shouldn't charge PAYG:

- **Price buyers.** As I said before the worst type of students are those whose main concern is to get the cheapest deal around. Not the best tuition or even the fairest price for first class tuition, just the cheapest. These students will not only drag down the niveau of your school, but also abandon you the

SHOW ME THE MONEY!

moment your competitors drop their prices. What's worse is that they will even bad mouth you because you are "expensive".

- **No time off.** Teaching martial arts is extremely rewarding but can also be tiring especially if you teach several hours per day five days per week. Like any human being you need time off to recuperate and relax. This is of course even more pressing if you have a family to look after. With PAYG you don't get paid if you don't teach. This puts you under enormous financial pressure to be as available as much as possible to your students, which is one reason why many don't want to teach full-time, especially as you get older.

- **No longevity.** Earlier on we talked about the importance of your vision for the business and in which direction you wish to take it in the years to come. Perhaps you might like to build the school up and pass it on to a senior student and focus on something different like writing or just doing the seminar circuit. Charging PAYG means that once you stop teaching, your students stop coming. There is very little you might be able sell or pass on in terms of an established business that is worth anything.

- **High student turn over.** You might be forgiven for thinking that PAYG is good for your students as they don't lose out if they don't train. But that is not so. PAYG actually encourages your students to stop training the moment they find a convenient excuse. And as there is no commitment from their side to pay; it's "bye-bye Sensei" long before they get anywhere near Black Belt. Although you might have quite a few people starting you essentially leave the back door wide open for students to leave at a whim. This is not only disappointing for you and the student as you now have helped them to fail to reach their training goal, but it is also financially risky as your rent, bills, etc., still need paying.

- **Dealing with money.** Apart from everything else PAYG will also drain off a lot of time from letting you get on with what you do best, that is teaching martial arts. If you have an average of twenty to thirty people attending your classes every night you will end up spending a significant amount of time running after your money and having to put up with excuses. In fact you will be perceived, by some students, as being only interested in money as you keep asking each one for their hard earned cash every night. And you will inevitably have to deal with those lovely chaps who are just waiting for an opportunity to cheat you out of a few quid because you forgot to ask them or because they haven't got their cheque book with them. Been there, done that, got the T-shirt and burned it!

CREDIT AGREEMENTS

For some, Credit Agreements are the work of the devil and a sure sign of "selling out". However, the moment I started to use them my membership base tripled within six months. It was only on the strength of knowing that there was a regular steady income that I dared to take on a full-time venue. I did however abandon this type of agreement for a while, which cost me dearly in student numbers as my attrition rate sky rocketed, which is why I went back to them.

For all the above mentioned reasons, I would never go back to PAYG credit agreements. They aren't a panacea and students still leave if they want to. Some critics would tell you that they would bring your school into disrepute as former students would inevitably hold them against you. Although I can see where they are coming from, I still think that people will always blame anyone but themselves for quitting.

BILLING COMPANIES

Billing companies especially for martial arts schools are another influence from our American cousins, which have sadly gained a bit of a bad rep in the industry. I have been a client of one that went against the wall whilst taking most of their clients' hard earned subscription payments with them. Thankfully I got rid of them a few months before they disappeared. Many like to be a one-stop-shop and offer you a whole host of services from the collection of your members' fees to training and teaching materials. It's always best to shop around and ask some probing questions and if possible speak to some of their existing and ideally former clients. Facebook, LinkedIn and/or Twitter should help you with your research. Don't expect that any of their staff have had experience running a school themselves, but they can serve as a useful networking tool to meet other like minded school owners.

Again, make sure to have a good look around if you consider employing a billing company to collect membership fees especially when it comes to their cut for collecting your money. Some will try to charge you up to ten percent on your total collectibles without any upward limit. This means that the more you make the more they keep without an increase of the services rendered to you (also referred to as the law of diminishing returns). A total rip off if you ask me. Try to find someone who can offer you a fixed amount per transaction, ideally a company which doesn't exclusively deal with martial arts schools. You might get asked to pay for a credit license which, at the time of writing, costs around £435 for a five year license.

Luckily, there only have been a few incidents where billing companies have gone into liquidation with a couple of months of their clients money still owing. This is perhaps one of the biggest downsides to the martial arts industry not being regulated in the UK.

One of the really great advantages of having a third party collecting money owed to you is that you will save a lot of time and hassle and it will allow you to get on with running a profitable school. Just imagine what it would do to your time management if you had to personally ensure that all of your 100 students have paid on time. I'm not saying billing companies are hassle free, but it's easier to deal with one from time to time than multiple headaches from reluctant students. Also when there are disputes you can use the billing company to mediate and thereby avoid making it personal. Apart from all that it also makes you look much more professional. Give me a billing company any time of the day.

There are other alternatives to credit agreements and billing companies. Some instructors get help from their partner and you are a lucky person if you should find such a fine person to help you in that way. If your better half doesn't want to know you can always employ someone part-time to act as your finance department. Outsourcing is great but I would still prefer a separate company to act on my behalf.

CARD PAYMENTS

If you are not accepting card payments you are really missing a trick! I sometimes jokingly say that our card machine is the most important piece of equipment in our school and I certainly wouldn't want to do without it anymore. It is very rare that anybody these days would carry large amounts of cash with them to pay for anything, least of all martial arts training. Remember that for many, choosing to do martial arts training at your school is not a rational decision at all and if people decide to join your school for whatever reason the last thing you want to do is to send them away to get cash or even their cheque book. In fact, if somebody says that they are just going to pop out to get cash it's usually just a polite or perhaps desperate attempt to avoid commitment. You will probably never see them again. Just for the record, we offer all new members a thirty-day money back guarantee, so they can pay with peace of mind. This is called risk reversal and is a great way to remove buying objections even if the blond banker is going to get her way in the end.

If you are not already using a card machine, you probably wouldn't believe how much business is conducted via card payments. I regularly sell hundreds of pounds worth of training that would be almost impossible to secure if it wasn't so convenient to pay by card.

Regardless of your current level of operation, do yourself a favour and please get a card machine. It's simple; all you have to do is to talk to your bank and they will lease you one for a monthly charge. As the market is quite competitive, ask them to waive any set-up charges, I did and they just dropped it. On top, you will be charged per transaction by the service provider.

Special Tip:
If you are roaming get hold of a mobile card payment machine. This will ensure that it is easy for your students and their parents to pay you. You need a merchant account for these.

There is a cool new gadget, which is currently being introduced into the UK, called iZettle (www.izettle.com), which allows you to accept card payments through your iPhone, iPad or iPod touch. All you need is a small card swipe attachment that plugs into your phone. No merchant account needed.

A word of caution. For some reason American Express charges a premium for each transaction that is much higher than any of the other card companies, like Visa or MasterCard. Having been stung by them before, I would be reluctant to accept those again in the future.

Paid In Full (PIF)

The way I offer training at our school, much like any college or university, is as a course which has a fixed price. This allows the student a lot more payment options, as they know exactly how much their training course costs them. Students and parents can budget and pay off their tuition faster if they wish. Charging like this makes the entire transaction more transparent for both sides and will seriously improve your cashflow situation.

If somebody wants to split their tuition into several big instalments (usually two to five) we use what we call a PIF sheet (see website for template). On it agree the number of instalments and amounts and get authorisation from your member to take the payments at an agreed date(s) without them having to be there. This way you don't have to keep chasing and reminding them that they still owe you money. Card machines give you the option to process payments while the card holder is absent.

Avoid the following mistakes:

- **Can't use, won't use.** If staff members are not confident enough to operate card machines, it usually means they haven't been trained well enough. This will cost you money every time.
- **A stitch in time.** Ensure you call your service provider ASAP if anything is wrong with the equipment. Regularly check if you still have sufficient paper rolls for the card machine.
- **Stocked up.** Ensure to have a good stock of PIF forms handy and that any staff members are trained to use them, especially if they are doing enrolments and upgrades.

RAPID RECAP – SHOW ME THE MONEY

- Your pricing strategy will affect the whole of your business and the kind of students you attract – so make sure you price according to your goals rather than just to undercut rivals.
- Be as flexible as possible in the way people can pay you without getting caught up in chasing individual payments. Use third party collections and card payments options to get paid faster, which leaves more time for you to get on with the real business of teaching and marketing.
- Believe in your prices and remember that people associate price with value.
- Remember in business cash flow is king. If you run out of money to pay your bills you are done. Reconsider especially smaller purchases as they tend to add up.
- Avoid PAYG at all cost.
- The only way to earn more money is to ask for it!

FINANCIAL MANAGEMENT

MANAGING CASH FLOW

"Happiness is a positive cash flow."
FRED ADLER

To effectively manage all the money that goes through your hands is a vital skill in running a profitable school. Some business people even claim that it is more important than knowing how to market and sell you products and services. Although I think that would perhaps be a bit of an exaggeration, consider this: if you lose a student, you can always go out, do a promotion and get a couple of new ones and work harder to keep these ones, but if you fail to have enough money to pay your suppliers, creditors or your employees you are out of business!

Understanding cash flow is the first step in managing your cash flow. There is a bit more to it than a fancy name for the movement of your money. Cash flow basically describes all movement in and out of your hands/bank accounts, including cash, cheques any card any card payments as well as loans and overdraft facilities from your bank on one hand and any and every bit of money going out including personal expenses and stamps on the other.

Looking ahead and understanding what your costs and liabilities are, at least one month ahead, is an important part of keeping a good cash flow going to ensure that you have more money coming than going out. The longer you plan ahead the better, but be aware that there will always be unplanned and unexpected expenditures. It is therefore a good idea to always have a bit of cash stashed away just in case. I would not rely on any bank to prop up your school as they are, by experience, only interested in their own balance sheet and not some fledging martial arts school. I'm proud of the fact that in all my eight years plus of operation I have never had a bank loan or even an overdraft facility on my business account.

TAX AND BOOK KEEPING

"The only two certainties in life are death and taxes."
MARK TWAIN

Whatever your views on paying taxes, I would recommend that you embrace the subject rather than avoid it. Do yourself a favour and create those positive pro-active habits right from the start and discipline yourself to do your bookkeeping regularly every week. This way you maintain a good overview on how your business is doing without being flattered by turnover and consequently are able to implement what changes you need to make. As I have mentioned earlier, you can only control something that you can actually measure. Remember: if you are not controlling your business then something or someone else is.

At this point you would also need to look into engaging an accountant who will file your annual tax returns. Don't be shocked if an accountancy firm quotes you anything from £600 upwards per year for doing your annual tax returns. Being a bigger or more prestigious firm doesn't mean they are necessarily doing a better job, they just like to charge more. The job of a decent accountant is to save you money year on year and not simply to add you to their long list of clients and merely to push a few buttons for you come the time of your tax return. You need to shop around and best network with other small business owners to get somebody recommended.

I would personally not recommend using software to DIY your tax return as tax legislation constantly changes and an experienced professional should always understand and actively exploit any legal tax loopholes for you, better than any software programme could ever do. Doing it yourself would also mean to skill up in that direction which would detract from the job in hand – attracting and keeping students.

Many novice school owners go through what seems like repeated annual experiences without ever learning from last year's mistakes and/or successes. This is often the result of bad or non existing record keeping. As a one-man-band you are probably not going to be of much interest to the Inland Revenue, however with a view to building a solid business there really is no excuse for trying to blag it.

Here are some tips that will make book-keeping a lot more efficient.

1. **Be Consistent**

   Consistency is essential to successful business book-keeping. If you use a paper book-keeping system, always be sure to head your columns the same way each month throughout the year. This small matter of consistency will save you and your accountant time and aggravation.

2. **Keep An Audit Trail**

   An audit trail is nothing more than a record of all your invoices and cheques in numeric order. The thing to remember is never skip numbers. Record voided cheque and invoice numbers in numeric order with all other cheques and invoices, only denote each one that is "voided." This assures there will be no gaps in your numerical sequence and leaves a proper audit trail.

3. **Keep Good Records**

   Many martial arts school owners don't keep good records. Some don't understand book-keeping; others understand it, but may be afraid of what the numbers might tell them. Think of it this way – book-keeping is the glue that keeps your business together. If your records aren't in good shape, the business could fall apart. A healthy business is monitored through its records on a regular basis so you can find problems and correct them before it's too late.

4. **You Are Taxed On Profits**

Many business owners think that they are taxed on all the money they take out of their business. In fact if you are a sole trader as opposed to a limited company (Ltd.) you are only taxed on your profits and not your turnover. Your accountant should be able to tell in advance what your tax liability might be for the past tax year. Make sure to put away a little money every month for your tax bill.

5. **VAT Worries**

From the 1st of April 2012 the threshold for VAT registration has been raised to £77,000 turnover per year. The good news is that in the UK all sports training and education services are still VAT exempt, provided these operate as a non-profit making organisation. According to the HMRC website[2] this would also include all non-profit martial arts training clubs. So, if you are a charitable organisation, you are exempt. If not you would still have to take over £6000 per month to even qualify to pay this tax, which in some ways is a problem you might like to have. Please contact your accountant if you have any concerns regarding your tax liabilities and/ or exemptions.

6. **Maintain Daily Records**

Think about it, if you don't have time to do a little book-keeping every day when will you have the time to do a week's or even a month's worth of records? Different people use different record keeping systems, what matters most is that you have a system and that you use it daily. We use a simple "Spider Chart" at our school, in which we record all our daily takings. All our receipts and invoices are kept in a filing tray and are collected and processed weekly. You can download a free Spider Chart template here www.martialartsbusinessschool.com/downloads

7. **Computer Software**

The biggest mistake people make is not taking enough time setting their accounting software up correctly when they install it on their computers. The old adage "Garbage in garbage out" applies here. If you want a financial report you can trust you have to make sure to set it up correctly to start with. I use a simple Excel spreadsheet for my book keeping, which I email my accountant every month. For a free book keeping template visit this book's website.

RAPID RECAP – FINANCIAL MANAGEMENT

- You can only control what you can measure. Make sure to become a friend of numbers and discipline yourself to keep good records.
- Cash flow is king in business. If you run out of money to pay your bills and suppliers you are done.
- There will always be unplanned expenditures. Make sure to build reserves for rainy days.
- Taxes are unavoidable. Have enough money put aside to pay your taxes at the end of the financial year.
- Only outsource book-keeping once you have a good understanding of what goes in and out of your business. Keep your finger on the pulse to avoid nasty surprises.

EXTRA STREAMS OF INCOME

"If you going to dream you might as well dream big."
WALT DISNEY

Most instructors and/or school owners leave a lot of money on the table, or rather on the mat, every month. That is they are either unaware of the multiple income streams the school or club offers, or are somewhat complacent about opportunities to ask for money.

Your income vastly depends on how much you think you need to make every month.

Be ambitious and set yourself income targets. Aim high and make your desired income your actual target amount. Once you have placed and/or raised the bar, look at the different ways you can increase your monthly income. However, don't be desperate or greedy; rather approach future income with an attitude of abundance and opportunity.

Relying on a single stream of income like your training fees for example, is very short-sighted and doesn't make any business sense. Please keep in mind that as far as your students are concerned if they continue to have a vested interest (time and money) in your services they are far more likely to stay and complete their training goals. As the saying goes, if they pay they stay.

It is a pretty reliable warning sign, that if a student becomes reluctant to spend any money on anything but training fees they are on their way out.

As a side note: You might be shocked at the thought to actually get rid of students, but if they are starting to spoil other people's fun and enjoyment by bickering and complaining they are directly undermining you and your efforts to create a great training environment and hence need to go, sooner rather than later.

In essence there are only three ways in which you can get paid more.

- You either have more students paying you your current rate – "Bums on seats."
- You have the same students paying more – Price increase.
- Or you get existing students to pay you more often – Increased value offers.

But no matter what you choose to do, in the end you must remember one single most important thing and that is to ask for the money.

Here are ten different ways that will help to generate additional income from your school, apart from your regular monthly member tuition fees.

PRIVATE TUITION

PT's are an excellent tool to cement your relationship with individual students, to fast forward them to black belt level, prepare them for gradings and to pre-frame them to upgrades. As there are only a finite number hours that you can be available during any given day to teach your time is limited and hence valuable. Don't sell yourself cheap, I know of some instructors who still charge £10 for an hour of private tuition. Remember what I said earlier about being reassuringly expensive. Students also pay for the privilege of training with the main man.

If you get too much demand either put your prices up or pass the session down to one of your assistant instructors, if you have any. Remember not to be too accessible, as you will reduce the exclusivity and hence the value of those sessions.

SEMINARS

Seminars can either be done internally or externally, that is to say you can be visiting other schools (your own, or someone else's) or do them in your own locale. Depending on your student count I would recommend you to make them an event and space them out over the year. Conducting a seminar every month in the same place will reduce the number of attendees as your students will assume that another one will be on next month anyway and end up pacing themselves.

GRADINGS

Grading or graduations are an absolute must and should not be left up to students to decide when they think they are ready. If a student is invited to a grading event, then that should suffice as a pre-qualification. It's up to you to clarify this from the outset. If they miss a grading for any reason, don't get tempted to offer private gradings too readily. Try to keep them something special. Some students insist on doing private gradings as they might feel too self conscious in front of others, but I believe that to be part of the grading ritual, which gives each student the feeling they've earned their next belt. Grading fees should not be included in any membership fees and as a rule of thumb should be charged at around 50% of the monthly training cost, for example £30 per grading if they pay £60 per month. Remember to apply any price increases only to new students as they don't know any different.

EQUIPMENT SALES

As a rule don't allow students or their parents to buy their own equipment. Inevitably some people will end up getting the cheapest bargains on eBay, which might not be fit for purpose and the whole class is starting to look like a martial arts theme party, which is not the image you want to go for as the premier training centre in your town. If you are a soft touch on that you are not only losing out financially but also with regards to branding. The best way around this is to get all your equipment including uniforms labelled or printed up with your school logo and sell everything out of your Pro-Shop. If you haven't got a full-time location, set-up an online store.

UNIFORMS/TEE-SHIRTS/MERCHANDISE

It is only normal for your members to want to identify with your "corporate identity". This branding of your school affords you a lucrative merchandising opportunity, which does not only give you free advertising but also additional income. There are almost no limits as to what you can offer your students to show their brand loyalty. The obvious items include uniforms, T-shirts, hoodies, sparring equipment like boxing gloves, kit bags, baseball hats, beanies, etc., but other things like mouse mats, car stickers, coffee mugs, calendars will also sell, provided there are visibly on offer in your Pro-Shop.

UPGRADES

If you are not already doing this you should definitely consider offering different courses for different levels of training, at different prices. These can make all the difference to the success of your school.

The benefits of having a progressive upgrade path for your students lie in the fact that most people like to know what else is out there once they have become comfortable and/or proficient in their current programme. This not only helps to keep students' enthusiasm high as they have something to look forward to, it also works as a great recruitment tool for home-grown future instructors that can help you to expand.

In order to ensure your students are kept interested and informed about what else you have offer, you need to keep talking about the benefits of theses training courses as well as having other already upgraded students talk about them in front of the class. The effect of these testimonials should not be underestimated as they provide you and your programmes with social proof, which acts as a powerful endorsement and motivation. This constant reminder of the other higher programmes (you never want to downgrade anyone) is called "pre-framing" and should be part of your ongoing teaching methodology. If, let's say, you run a Black Belt club, a Leadership programme or an Instructors course you need to draw attention to the fact that, for example doing a technique or form in a certain way shows "black belt attitude". Or that by attending every session, seminar and grading a student displays the required level of commitment that would pre-qualify him/her to be invited to the next programme. The fact that all your training is on an invitation basis only, creates an element of scarcity and hence exclusivity, which increases the perceived value of such training programmes. These courses must be of a higher value and offer a marked increase in training that should be in stark contrast to the basic training course. A visible indicator such as different colour uniforms, or at least a badge on their training top, can be used very effectively as an upgrade tool.

The basic course must therefore be just that – basic – with two sessions maximum per week on fixed training days with short classes of no longer than forty-five minutes. These sessions should be designed as an introduction to martial arts and to build up confidence and fitness to prepare new students for proper training. The beginner's course could be seen as a recruitment pool that enables you to identify the most dedicated and committed candidates that you can take all the way to black belt.

Don't make the mistake of giving it all away in the first instance. Not only is it wasted on most novices, as they have no way to appreciate your level of expertise (why would they come to you otherwise?), but it also leaves very little to the imagination and therefore nothing to look forward to.

Once you have identified and spoken to a prospective higher student about the level of training, present them with a printed invitation or acceptance to the higher programme in front of the entire class and get their fellow students to acknowledge their achievement through a round of applause. I have had some students almost in tears of joy, gladly accepting and paying for the privilege of being accepted to the Black Belt club.

To mark the commitment to a higher level of training every successive course must be priced at a higher rate and also should include a down payment. I charge an initial £500 down payment to upgrade to our Black Belt club and Leadership programme.

It's in understanding and applying these upgrade dynamics that you will catapult the success of your school to previously unknown heights.

Beginners should start on a basic programme or a foundation course and then upgrade into a higher programme when they are invited to join.

COURSES

Courses should not be confused with seminars. The great thing about teaching martial arts is the broad appeal to so many different audiences. Specialist courses can include: general self defence, self defence for women, weapons, ground fighting, kid's safety, restraint and control techniques, etc. They are a great recruitment tool and give you extra income as well.

CASH-OUTS

In business cash flow is king, especially when hit by unexpected bills and expenditures. I give my students the option to pay up for their training costs in advance in return for a proportional discount. This affords them considerable savings and allows me to buy much need equipment, get a much deserved holiday or create a nest egg by investing or saving money. The reason why I can do that is that I offer a fixed cost for my students training much like a college course. The danger with cash-outs is for you to enjoy the sudden influx of cash a bit too much and to offer this payment option to too many members, which can result in a much reduced monthly income. Another way is to offer selective members a fast-pay option in which they can pay off their course cost in twelve months instead of three years, again in return for a discount saving. This can of course also be applied to grading fees and seminar bundles.

ENROLMENT FEES

Once a prospective student qualifies to get accepted into your school or course, an enrolment fee should be applied. I currently charge £99 pounds for people enrolling into my school. Apart from their first month of training, this also gives the students their licence, membership, insurance as well as their basic uniform. Supplying a uniform is optional and can later be part of the much needed equipment pack. It is important psychologically that students need to pay "pain money"; a certain amount that registers with them as a commitment. I have seen many occasions where students were even allowed to train for free without any financial commitment whatsoever, which only resulted in them turning their back as it was seen as "cheap" and available and hence worthless. It takes superior dedication and willpower to throw yourself into a (part-time) training regime without getting side-tracked or distracted by events or life in general. Ever joined a gym and didn't end up going?

Most people also do not understand the value of what you have to offer and will inevitably judge you based on price, as this is their current frame of reference. As marketing consultant and author Dan Kennedy said: "Your clients have no way to evaluate your expertise. In most professional services you are not selling your expertise as it is assumed and the prospect cannot intelligently evaluate your expertise anyway."

It is therefore your job to highlight the value and benefits (not the features) of your training to potential trainees. An enrolment fee makes membership of your school or club more exclusive and thus more valuable in the mind of the prospect. There is no doubt that it will put off some people, but we have already talked about price buyers.

Don't short-change yourself by making yourself too available, it won't make you more popular.

PASSIVE INCOME

This is perhaps one of the most important forms of income as you only have to do the work once and then pretty much forget about it. Set-up correctly it enables people to buy your information products online or via your Pro-Shop. Books, DVDs and online content make very good passive income streams.

RAPID RECAP - EXTRA STREAMS OF INCOME

- Once you've established your school there are many ways to increase the income you can generate from each customer while providing an even better experience.
- Unless you like leaving money on the table you need to work these additional income streams into your business as early as possible.
- Equipment and training do not sell themselves; you have to give students/parents a reason to buy additional things by selling them the benefits first.
- Make sure everybody knows what is on offer by advertising and talking about it before, during and after class as well as in newsletters.

TEACHING AND CLASS MANAGEMENT

"A teacher must never impose his student to fit his favourite pattern. A good teacher functions as a pointer, exposing his student's vulnerability (and) causing him to explore both internally and externally and finally integrating himself with his being. Martial arts should not be passed out indiscriminately."

BRUCE LEE

Becoming an instructor in a martial arts school is often a really exciting time because in many ways you feel like you have made it. In order to teach others you must have already mastered the basic content and now is your chance to "give back" your knowledge and continue the progression of your style.

This is a great honour but it is not without its pitfalls. As any experienced instructor knows, teaching martial arts, and practising martial arts, are in many ways two completely different skill sets. Simply because someone has earned a black belt doesn't automatically make them an expert teacher.

Teaching and educating people in a class or seminar environment, is a skill like any other and needs to be learned and practiced. When I made my first baby steps as a junior instructor I had no idea how to write a curriculum or lesson plan or even how to praise my students. It was simply a question of "monkey see, monkey does" and all I did was to copy my instructor down to the Lancashire accent that he spoke. I literally punched, kicked and choked my way through dozens of unsuspecting students and asked myself why nobody stayed. It wasn't until many years of trial and error that the penny dropped and I was able to take some students towards their black belt.

Here are five of the most common mistakes that new instructors can make.

If you are an experienced instructor reading this, please do not forget to relate some of your own teaching horror stories to your assistant instructors, so that they can learn from your mistakes as well.

ROOKIE MISTAKE 1: SHOWING UP TO CLASS WITHOUT A LESSON PLAN AND "WINGING IT"

This is a **BAD** idea for any new instructor. Planning is critical in all aspects of life and in any job. Being a martial arts instructor is no exception. Just because you are good at your chosen art, does not mean that you can instantly snap all of the instructor puzzle pieces together and teach an inspiring class without a lesson plan.

Even many experienced instructors refer to some type of lesson plan or overall structure before teaching each class. A lesson plan will guarantee that you are organized, that you do not "freeze" on the spot, and that you are not constantly thinking, "OK, what shall I do next?" When you are in this mode, it means that you are not focusing on your students in the moment!

Remember: You've heard the expression 'If you fail to plan you plan to fail'. Having even a sketchy plan or outline of your next class(es) will reduce stress and give you greater peace of mind. Students want to be reassured that they have come to the right place. Being prepared will make you look competent and trustworthy.

ROOKIE MISTAKE 2: TRYING TO TEACH EVERYTHING YOU KNOW IN ONE CLASS

It is very tempting as a new instructor to feel the need to stamp your authority on a class and to prove yourself to your group as being very knowledgeable. Consequently in your first class you drill your students in every possible basic technique, all of the different forms whether they know them or not, and multiple partner work drills to the point of overload. This causes major stress to your students as they will feel completely overwhelmed and when you go to teach your next class, you will not have anything new left to give them. There are very good reasons for a structured curriculum and a solid lesson plan.

Remember: The surest way to teach someone nothing is to teach them everything.

ROOKIE MISTAKE 3: TEACHING CLASS SO THAT YOU GET A GOOD WORKOUT

Stop being selfish! There is a difference between leading by example and training with your peers. In every class that you teach, your primary focus should be on the needs of your students and not on yours. In the end it's your students who are paying you to teach them and not to self-indulge. It will be inevitable that you will get a good workout just by demonstrating the different techniques, forms and partner work drills to your students, and it is important to model these things well.

Remember: You have to learn to become boring. To be able to teach the same material over and over again to hundreds of students over many years and to still look like you're having the time of your life is the hall mark of a great teacher. There is a great temptation to show off and to over-teach, using material that is beyond the physical level or comprehension of a student. This can happen because you might feel the urge that you still need to "convert" or convince your students or because you are somewhat bored with the basic beginner's curriculum (which is, of course, basic for a reason).

I don't mean that you should appear to be bored to your students, but to learn to be patient with teaching the same basic and perhaps boring material over and over again, whilst at the same time looking interested, motivated and that you are enjoying yourself. If you find that hard, simply fake it till you make it.

ROOKIE MISTAKE 4: BEING TOO HARD OR TOO EASY

There are very often two types of new instructors. Type one is the drill instructor who wants to put the students through hell so they know who is boss, and type two is the friend who wants everyone to like him and is overly nervous about how well he taught each class.

Try to find some middle ground and work your students hard by holding them to high standards, but also develop strong and respectful relationships with them and show them that you care about them and their success.

Remember: Your students ultimately don't care how much you know, but they know how much care. Don't try to impress them, but serve them and make each training session fun and memorable.

ROOKIE MISTAKE 5: ALLOWING YOUR STUDENTS TO DECIDE ON THE CONTENT FOR THE CLASS

This is a **BIG** mistake because so many things can go wrong. First, you cannot please everybody and by asking what your students want to study you will get requests for everything possible within any group – forms training, sparring, pad work and target training, and self-defence. You can't possibly fit everything into one class, nor should you (see mistake #2).

Also, don't entertain every question a student may have. The question may be relevant to the style or drill you are teaching but answering would not only throw you off your lesson plan, but also bore the other students. It's not uncommon for students to ask a question for the sake of asking, in order to get attention or sneak in a break from the exercise. By all means clarify a drill or form but keep questions to the end of the class.

Remember: You are the leader of the class and your students expect you to know what they need to study. Do not abdicate your responsibility to your students and allow them to dictate your content or methods in the class. This makes you look weak as a leader and you will lose control over the class.

CURRICULUMS

A curriculum is your roadmap in your efforts to take your students to black belt and beyond. A well-written curriculum not only represents a clear written statement of intent, it gives your teaching structure, purpose and direction and will motivate students as it clarifies their learning goals.

A well defined curriculum also protects the student from the teacher in that it should prevent any favouritism or impulsive urges, on the side of the instructor, to fall into "flavour of the month" sessions that may well be very entertaining but have no bearing on the particular learning objective of the student.

When you develop the learning objectives for each student grade it should undoubtedly lead to new insights into the purpose, content and delivery methods of your classes.

Learning objectives should describe the kind of performance expected by the learner at the end of each grade. It is unrealistic to expect every student to perform the same form or technique in the same way, especially when you take their age, experience, and physical ability into account. It is more realistic to expect each student to be able to perform the required material, determine if it has been carried out correctly and then to correct if it was not. I measure student performance on, what I call, "the three Cs" – Confidence, Comprehension, and Control. Performance elements such as attitude and (controlled) aggression should be kept for higher grades or extra credit.

A Word Of Caution

Adults and children have very different learning objectives and learn in very different ways to each other, which should never be confused. Kids' classes are typically shorter than adult classes and tend to be arranged around activities and games. A lot more emphasis should be placed on rewards in the form of stickers, patches and special belts when teaching children. There must be different curriculums for adults and kids classes.

It is important to understand that learning objectives are not necessarily set in stone. You may find that as you gain fresh insights into the purpose and methods for your class delivery, your view of the course goals and objectives may also change.

For example, when I first started teaching my style, Wing Chun, it was (and still is by many) predominantly taught around the various forms it contains. The applications were dictated by the forms, as every move was scrutinised after being taught. This perhaps more traditional approach, works very well in most cases. When I re-evaluated my curriculum however the overall purpose of learning Wing Chun, the learning of reality based self-defence, started to govern the way I set out each student grade in a progressive way. The end product was that I no longer modelled the applications around the forms, but used the positions and movements of the system to cater for the specific learning objective of each student grade. In this way the system was now serving the student needs and not vice versa.

Linear vs. Rotating

There are essentially two types of curriculum that are being used in martial arts tuition. The one that is perhaps more commonly used by traditional martial arts instructors is the Linear Curriculum, whereby a student is taken from white belt to black belt in an ABC fashion, where each grade builds on the previous one.

The other is called a Rotating Curriculum, which is not necessarily a new concept, but has gained popularity over recent years and is now used by many commercially successful schools.

It is different in that the student learns the student grade material according to when he/she joins the school. The material is taught in semesters which can be two or three month periods. Two-month semesters would be more suitable for kids' classes.

The key to this concept is that *everyone* will be learning the same material during that semester, whether they joined that month or three months ago. Most traditional instructors, who have been brought up on a linear curriculum will initially have trouble with this concept. They might find it difficult to imagine that a student who has been studying for six months is learning the same material as someone who just joined that month. It definitely takes some time to get used to, but experience shows that this sort of programme does work.

In response to those who might be concerned that this type of curriculum dilutes or cheapens rank, I would like to offer a different perspective. Remember that with a rotating curriculum, all students will know all the same techniques after twelve months of training. The main concern should hence be focused on the end result and not on who is training what at what time. After completion of year one, whether you call it "first level" or "blue belt" a student should have acquired the basics of your style or programme. A Rotating Curriculum will ensure that this happens.

A class could be divided in different phases, beginners, intermediate and advanced, or different groups can be taught in separate time slots, depending on availability and cost, if you are renting by the hour. This way allows an instructor to teach a maximum of three groups at any one time as opposed to a possible twelve.

Example: If, on a quarterly rotation, "Joe" joins in April at the beginning of the second rotation, he will have completed his basic programme around the same time the following year. He will then progress onto phase two, the intermediate level programme, etc. There should be a cut-off point, perhaps around week eight, for late comers to each rotation for this student to be asked to be tested on that material. Students can always be fast tracked via private sessions and seminars.

The following diagram illustrates the basic structure of the rotating curriculum.

A Quarterly Rotating Curriculum	First Year (Phase 1)	Second Year (Phase 2)	Third Year (Phase 3)
First Quarter (Jan-Mar)	GRADE 1 SYLLABUS	GRADE 5 SYLLABUS	GRADE 9 SYLLABUS
Second Quarter (Apr-Jun)	GRADE 2 SYLLABUS	GRADE 6 SYLLABUS	GRADE 10 SYLLABUS
Third Quarter (Jul-Sep)	GRADE 3 SYLLABUS	GRADE 7 SYLLABUS	GRADE 11 SYLLABUS
Fourth Quarter (Oct-Dec)	GRADE 4 SYLLABUS	GRADE 8 SYLLABUS	GRADE 12 SYLLABUS

The advantages of teaching a Rotating Curriculum are:
- Better class atmosphere.
  As everyone is working together it creates a greater communal atmosphere in the class.
- Greater motivation.
  New students feel happier to work with more senior students, who can help them with the basics as everyone practices the same material.
- Better time management
  for the instructor. As he/she doesn't have to split his/her time and attention into ten or more different programmes it makes it much easier for a single instructor to look after a larger class.

LESSON PLANS

As mentioned before, being adequately prepared for each lesson is crucial, especially for new or junior instructors, but many seasoned instructors can also benefit from it. As planning removes any guess-work as to what or how long to teach a particular skill set, instructors can focus more on the needs of the students. This level of control and confidence will reflect in your body language and will make you look more competent, even if you are more nervous, which is normal for new instructors. A lesson plan should not only help you with your time management and content discipline, it should also give you a better understanding of what equipment, if any, you might need or could use to help you teach particular skills, or to make the class more interesting and fun. If you have a special session planned you can then also ask students to bring things that might help them enjoy and or retain more of your session. If, for example you are planning an extended workout or sparring session you could ask students to bring an additional T-shirt. If, on the other hand you like to focus more on theory, students should bring their note pads.

Class Structures

A class should be structured around the specific needs and abilities of the student(s) and follow specific learning objectives. The way the instructor should structure a class is to ensure that there is no downtime for the students and that the students are kept actively engaged from beginning to end. A well-structured lesson plan is an absolute must to keep a class free from distractions and guesswork.

As a rule, beginners' classes should be high intensity with very little talking or explaining on either side. Questions should be kept for the end of the session so they do not interrupt the flow of the class.

Advanced classes on the other hand should be of lower intensity with more room to explain advanced concepts and to absorb more complex ideas. Questions are important here as they indicate the level of comprehension of the student.

Each class should be segmented into different drills and activities as this helps to establish a familiar flow and rhythm for the student. Each item on your lesson plan shouldn't take up more than five to ten minutes of your class and should contribute towards the overall objective of the session. If too little time is spend on an item, students might get confused as to the point of it, if you spend too long on it they might get bored.

A class should typically start off with a light warm-up or joint mobilisations to allow increased blood flow to these areas. Depending on the emphasis and nature of the class the warm-up can increase and lead into pad drills to energise the class. The core of the class might be a bit slower as new skills and ideas maybe introduced. The end of a class should be high energy again, perhaps leading to some stretching and a little time right at the end for theory, questions or announcements.When introducing a new skill or element it should first be introduced by demonstrating the drill or technique and key points should be explained. The skill should then be broken down into simple incremental steps and practised. At the end of the session it should be reviewed and room for feedback and questions should be made. Remember to keep the introduction and review short, sharp and to the point.

Hiding Repetition
Martial arts training, in its very nature, requires endless repetition for a skill to become part of one's muscle memory so that it can eventually be mastered. Many students don't make it past the beginning stages as they get bored by endless repetition, especially when compared to other more exiting competitive sports. The trick is to hide or disguise repetition to keep the students interested and motivated. This can be done in many different ways, mainly by changing or adding key elements of a familiar routine.

Drills, forms and applications can be spiced up by changing the order in which they are done, by adding a time limit or a weapon, or with the addition of a creative element by asking students to come up with a warm-up routine, for example.

Networking with other instructors and visiting other martial arts schools can go a long way in getting fresh ideas to keep you inspired and motivated which will rub off, on to your students.

Class Durations

The conventional wisdom for the length of a regular evening class is typically around sixty to ninety minutes and sometimes even as long as two hours, regardless of fitness level or ability of the students. This is what I did when I started and practised for many years. As I mentioned before, we tend to see the world from our perspective and just because we might have been brought up in a certain way doesn't make this the way to go in the future.

In an effort to provide value for money some instructors might think that more is better. In the same way that you shouldn't drown your students in information, longer classes are in no way a guarantee for being better classes. More is often just more and a well-structured shorter session can help and enthuse the students just as much if not more so. From a newcomer's point of view the prospect of a ninety minute gruelling martial arts session (of which half of it is often just callisthenics) can be an instant turn off. Nobody wants to look like a fool or an unfit couch potato in front of others.

For this reason all newbies to our school are put into a forty five minute beginner's session to ease them into the world of martial arts. The classes are non-stop and high intensity with very little talking or explaining. Students get a nice workout, learn a part of a form, one technique or application and usually leave the session happy, energised and wanting more. This format allows the students enough time and energy to also enjoy the remaining evening with their friends and families. Once these beginners have been coming for a few months they are ready to be upgraded into a higher programme with longer sessions, which shouldn't exceed sixty minutes. Anything longer than this and students will begin to clock-watch or create their own water and toilet breaks. Keep intensive training sessions as special occasions, which can last as long as five or six hours, perhaps with an opportunity to grade at the end.

A-Days and B-Days
Depending on the amount of different skills and drills your students need to learn for their next grading you could also plan to have different lesson plans for different training days. This allows you to break classes down even further by focusing on different things on different days. An A-day could be a Monday and/or a Tuesday and a B-day a Wednesday and/or Thursday class. A-days could be focused on introducing new material and B-days on practicing the new material.This format has the following benefits:
- You don't have to fit everything into a single class and therefore have more time to focus on a specific drill or form.
- It gives less experienced instructors a simpler formula to follow when constructing lesson plans.
- It allows students to catch up on specific aspects of training they might have missed.

Special Training Events
Beyond your regular weekly sessions there are plenty more things you can offer to your students to enhance their learning experience and to offer value for money. The thing to remember here is that these need to work towards your overall training objectives and school ethos and shouldn't interfere with them.

Special training events can include seminars, open classes or clinics, summer camps, workshops, tournaments, specialist courses, e.g. on self-defence or weapons, special guest instructor sessions or workshops, charity board breaking events, outdoor training, etc.

Nothing sucks quite like a badly attended event especially if you have invited the local paper to cover it. So remember to plan these well in advance and give students plenty of notice so they can schedule your events into their busy lives. Announce them regularly in class, on notice boards, websites and newsletters. Avoid making unannounced or short notice changes, as it breaks trust and rapport and will have a knock-on effect on future events.

If you plan a kids' event, always sent an accompanying letter to the parents as they are used to this from the schools their children attend. Also make sure that you get parents to sign release forms if you are planning to use any pictures you take during those events on your websites or on any promotional material.

RAPID RECAP – TEACHING AND CLASS MANAGEMENT

- Being a black belt doesn't automatically make you an instructor.
- Planning your classes and courses is the bread and butter of any instructor worth his salt.
- A good teacher is never selfish and always puts the interests and needs of his/her students first.
- A well-written curriculum is your roadmap to teaching success.
- Adults and children have different learning objectives and should never be taught in the same class.
- Rotating curriculums are used by many commercially successful schools.
- Lesson plans ensure proper time management and content discipline.
- Less is more when it comes to class duration.
- Hiding repetition keeps students interested and motivated.
- Special training events need to be advertised in as many ways as possible to ensure good turnouts.

KEEPING STUDENTS HAPPY ...
AND COMING BACK FOR MORE

*"There is only one boss. The customer. And he can fire
everybody in the company from the chairman on down, simply
by spending his money somewhere else."*
SAM WALTON, FOUNDER OF WAL-MART

All your marketing and sales skills are pretty meaningless if you
can't hold on to your students. Imagine that all the inquiries and
enrolments you generate through your marketing efforts as water
that goes into a bucket which is riddled with holes. A lot goes in but
nothing stays for very long. If that sounds familiar then you have a
serious conversion and/or retention problem.

NATURAL VERSUS AVOIDABLE ATTRITION AND
HOW TO PLUG THE LEAKS

Good and consistent customer service should give you the tools to
plug (most of) these leaks and help you to convert most of the
prospects you attract into long-term paying students. This process
is also referred to as streamlining the life cycle of your students. You
can easily find out for certain if you have a lot of holes in your
customer service bucket by looking at your attrition rate. The
attrition rate is the percentage of students you lose month by month.
An attrition rate that is considered "normal" for our industry is
between 4%-7%, that means that for every ten students you have,
you are likely to lose one every other month. The more students you
have, the more people you are likely to have to replace every month.
At a hundred students per month you have to recruit six new

students every month just to keep your students count static. If you want to grow, you obviously need to enrol more than you lose. If your attrition rate is under 4% you are in fact doing well. If it is around 10% or more you need to take drastic and immediate action.

There were times when we, at our school in Norwich, lost more students per month than we do now. The reason for this is that we have managed to plug most of the holes that caused us to haemorrhage students, and therefore time and money. This I believe is a sign of the times as the current economic situation forces you to look after your existing students a lot more. This is because it is much harder to attract new ones as disposable income is not what it used to be only three or four years ago. That is prior to the market crash in 2008 and the double dip recession which is biting at the time of writing.

Whatever the economic climate, there is really no substitute for building genuine relationships with every individual student if you want them to continue to train with you and even recommend others to come along and to give you a try. You want to build up a reputation not only for being *the* local expert in your area but also for the way you look after your students so that they will be recommending you to all their friends and families. This of course must also extent to all visitors and students parents if you teach children.

In the life cycle of a student, it is important for you to understand that nobody stays forever, meaning that everybody eventually leaves, and it is hence your job to draw out that point of departure. People start martial arts training for their own reasons and will stop for their own reasons. Even if you do everything right 100% of the time, your students will still leave at some point. Don't take it personally. In the vast majority of cases it has more to do with a change in their circumstances, such as a new/no job, new relationship, moving home, etc., than anything you may or may not have done. This, of course, does not mean that you can afford to be complacent. Apart from trying to increase what is on offer at your school like fitness classes or special events, it is really the little things that make all the difference to your students. Remember: Your students really don't care how much you know until they know how much you care.

Here are ten things you can do to improve and enhance your students' experience of your school without breaking the bank:

1. **Postcards**. Send out postcards to your members for their birthdays, when they are off sick and even once they have passed their next grading. The cost for each postcard is virtually nothing but students really appreciate the fact that you show that you care. You can get martial arts-specific postcards from www.merit-badges.com.

2. **Newsletters**. Mail out a school newsletter via email to promote events, student achievements and to introduce or review new products, courses, etc. you can use services like www.constantcontact.com, www.mailchimp.com or aweber.com.

3. **Thank you letters**. Send out thank you letters and/or welcome packs to new students once they have enrolled in your school. A short note to tell them how much you value their trust in you and your services and a few beginners' tips can go a long way in providing additional motivation and even a referral.

4. **Phone skills**. If you take your own calls (we use a professional answering service) then practice professional etiquette and mannerisms. Here are some professional phone etiquettes you need to practice:
   a) Try to answer each call within no more than three rings.
   b) Always answer the phone by using your name in the initial greeting.

c) If you need to place callers on hold ask them for permission first and wait for them to give you their consent before doing so.

d) When taking details over the phone always repeat them back to them, especially phone numbers and email addresses.

e) Make sure to be polite and attentive and always thank them for calling you.

5. **Assign each new trainee a training buddy**. Everybody dreads feeling awkward in front of other people especially if they are new. Having a training buddy means that they have somebody who can show them the ropes and help them to feel welcome and at ease much sooner. Make sure it's someone of their age and ability; being stuck with a black belt can be intimidating.

6. **Accept card payments**, direct debits and online payments options. I have already mentioned the benefits of doing that in the chapter Show Me The Money. The easier and more convenient it is for your students to pay you the more likely it is for you to be paid on time and in full.

7. **Offer a no hassle money back guarantee**. This is called "risk reversal" and gives the student the extra peace of mind that they can back out if they have to. Make sure that you limit the guarantee to the initial enrolment fee or the first month of training and don't leave yourself open to abuse.

8. **Provide payments options**. Most students will want to pay in monthly instalments, some might prefer to pay up front for six months or a year and others like to pay as they train. If they cash-out their membership or programme, offer a discount as an incentive or reward. Remember not to get suckered in by pay as you go payments.

9. **Offer payments freeze**. Try to accommodate your students as much as possible even if they might have difficulties paying for the odd month. We offer to freeze their payments for a month if that's the case. It can make your life a bit easier if you have a billing company to arrange and control your payments especially if you start having more than fifty students at any one time.

10. **Ease their departure**. On one hand you don't want to make it too easy for your students to leave whenever they feel like it and on other hand you don't want to leave a bad taste in their mouth by creating a hassle when they do. You don't want to make your students your enemies by forcing them to pay even if they no longer use your services. We ask our members to give us at least ninety days notice if they want to leave. If you part company amicably they might even return to continue their training one day.

Above all, be personable, approachable and easy going. A really good way to build rapport with students and to show them you care about them is the following method which has come out of my many years of dealing with students of all walks of life. I always try to remember three things about each and every student,

1. **Their name**. Everybody's favourite sound is the sound of hearing their own name. A great way to remember their name is to keep repeating it to them as much as possible without looking strange.

2. **Their occupation**. A rather useful bit of information, as it not only offers many points of chit chat and banter apart from the obvious subject of martial arts. It also tells you if there is perhaps the chance for a bit of bartering. I have traded countless sessions of personal training for services, deals and equipment over nearly twenty years that would have otherwise cost me a small fortune.

3. **The last topic of conversation.** Nothing works quite as smooth in building and maintaining sound rapport and an atmosphere where students feel they are liked and appreciated, as seamlessly picking up a conversation you had with them last time or to ask about something they told you about when you spoke to them last.

When is the last time you came to a sports club or your local pub where someone you like and respect not only calls out your name with a big smile on their face as you walked in, but also asked you how your day at the office was and (time permitting) even enquired about the holiday trip abroad that you have planned with your girlfriend for the last three months. Wouldn't you like going back there regularly as you are made welcome and part of the team? I'm not talking about some loud behaviour or fake high fives as this can have the opposite effect. Just think how you would like to be treated if the roles were reversed. If you think you might not be able to be quite as gregarious and extrovert as that, then role play situations until you can at least appear that you care about your students more than your closest competitor. As the saying goes: Fake it 'til you make it!

If you are one of those people who think that your memory barely allows you to remember your partners name and birthday and the PIN number of your bank card then you need to do some more training. Your memory, like your martial arts skills is like a muscle whose performance can be massively improved by training and drilling. Don't believe me? Check out "Your Memory: How It Works and How to Improve It." by Kenneth L. Higbee.

A dirty school, rude behaviour, a sudden hike in prices or constant changes in the timetable or instructor will drive out students faster than you can imagine.

Over the years I have heard stories about instructors who were getting their students to do their shopping, bullying students, chatting up students and their mums and even of some who were caught *in flagrante delicto* with their students on the mat! Apart from being flagrant violations of the student/teacher relationship, incidents like these will *Dim Mak* your reputation and are a stain on our calling as instructors. Keep them safe, keep them happy, keep them paying. Don't take liberties!

Thinking of Skipping This Stuff? Here Are Some Customer Services Stats To Make You Think Again

- For every customer complaint, there are twenty-six other customers who have remained silent.
- Happy customers tell at least four others about positive experiences, whereas dissatisfied customers will tell between nine and fifteen different people about their negative experience.
- A 2% increase in student retention has the same effect on profits as cutting costs by 10%.
- Attracting a new student costs five times more than keeping an existing one.
- 90% of online consumers worldwide trust recommendations from people they know and 70% trust consumer opinions posted online.
- Poor customer service is costing UK businesses £15.3 BILLION! every year. (Source: Genesys Telecommunications Laboratories Report – The Cost Of Poor Customer Service)

RECEPTION

The reception area in your school is a key area and should look clean and professional. It functions as the nerve centre of your school and must be kept neat and organised. The reception should be the place where people pay for training and equipment and should contain the cash register and card machine. Behind the reception area should be off limits to the general public and during opening hours must be constantly staffed by friendly and trained team members who can deal with any enquiry quickly and efficiently. These staff members should be able to do the following:

- Welcome new members and visitors.
- Book-in induction sessions and chase up cancelled and/or missed appointments.
- Do induction sessions and sell memberships.
- Know how to process all types of payments, including issuing refunds and calculating discounts as and when applicable.
- Fill in and process any paperwork for new enrolments.
- Deal with any billing enquiry or at least be able to escalate them to the right person.
- Handle complaints and cancelations and escalate issues to the right person.
- They should also be able to assist existing students with any training-related enquiries like dates for upcoming seminars and gradings, book in private tutorials and
- Assist with pro-shop and refreshment sales.
- Track attendance and deal with MIA calls, postcards and reactivation letters.

DEALING WITH COMPLAINTS

"Feedback is the breakfast of champions."
KENNETH BLANCHARD

Never be afraid or too proud to apologise. We are all human after all and nobody expects you to be perfect; you shouldn't either. Things will inevitably go wrong from time to time and students and/or their parents might complain. Don't be defensive or argumentative when somebody cares enough to complain to you. Look at complaints as vital feedback that give you the opportunity to address areas that have slipped your attention. Be grateful your customers actually take the time and make the effort to bring this to your attention. How many times have you just walked off if the service of a shop or restaurant has annoyed you?

You didn't care enough for the business to even tell them what rubbed you up the wrong way. Which means that they would have most likely continued to repeat the same mistake over and over again and put off a lot more customers like yourself. But what adds insult to injury is that if you do think they deserve to be told and you muster your courage and ask for the manager, and instead of dealing with your concern professionally and swiftly, he or she either gives some platitudes or, worst still argues with you trying to keep face. They are, of course, being utterly feckless, because not only will you not come back again, you will tell all your friends and family to avoid this place like a leper colony. Spurred on by your hurt feelings you will go one step further and slag them off on Facebook and Twitter as well. This is easily done by just whipping out your trusted little smart phone.

We live in a time of mass communications and all the big brands jealously defend their reputations, as the power is now in the hands of the little man who can start an effective smear campaign from his or her bedroom that costs nothing more than the time it takes to post their experiences on enough websites (remember Wikileaks?).

So when somebody cares enough and complains to you, welcome it and thank them for bringing this to your attention and helping you to improve your operation. If they are getting personal, don't respond in kind. Instead move the conversation into your office or a more private space. Let them vent a bit, acknowledge their frustration and then ask them what the issue is. The worst thing you can do at this point is to become defensive and to play the blame game. If the customer isn't about to calm down and unwilling to deal with the issue ask them how it is that you can help them resolve the issue, otherwise to come back once they have managed to calm down.

Above all, don't let one unhappy customer ruin your whole day. Take some time to reset before dealing with the next thing; you don't want to pass on the bad vibes to your other students and staff members. If an individual or a situation has upset you that much, take a few deep breaths or let off some steam on a punching bag before returning to face everybody else.

This is a tried and tested procedure to deal with a complaint:

- Listen to all they have to say without interrupting them or arguing with them. Maintain eye contact and make sure to give them your undivided attention.
- Then paraphrase what they have said to show them you have been listening and ask if you have understood their concerns correctly.
- If you can fix it now do so, without fuss and hesitation, and find a way to make it up to them in some way.
- After that, be sure to make your staff aware of what happened so they can avoid the same situation with others or even the same customer.
- If at all possible, get back to them and inform your customer what you have done to redress the situation.

STUDENT SURVEYS

"USA Today has come out with a new survey – apparently, three out of every four people make up 75% of the population."
DAVID LETTERMAN

Now people don't expect you to be perfect but they do expect you to fix things if they are not up to their expectations or perhaps not as you made them out to be. Remember to always under-promise and over-deliver.

The secret of outstanding customer service lies in the fact that everybody likes to be shown, not just told, that they are liked and that they matter. Just think how you would like to be treated if you were in their place. Things will start to go south once expectations are mismatched, which are almost always a result of bad communications. It is often the small things that make all the difference.

It is important that you keep your finger on the pulse and anticipate and react quickly to anything that might give your students any reason to depart prematurely.

So how do you know what your students really want? Well, the best thing is just to ask them. Customer surveys are a very powerful tool that you should use regularly to find out if there are any latent issues and also to take credit if you are doing a sterling job. You have the choice of either doing a paper or online version of your survey. You can use free online services like www.surveymonkey.com.

A survey can be used in two very specific ways. The first way is to assess each individual student's progress and training goals. In this case, students should provide their names on the survey.

The second way is to analyse the performance of your school in which case you can keep it anonymous. Instead, evaluate the questionnaire by demographics like age, gender, rank, etc., which can give you a contrast of how beginners vs. advanced students, or male vs. female students, or adult vs. children view and validate your school, its staff and its services.

The following is a survey I designed for my students. It should give you some ideas as to what to ask.

Sample Survey (assessing school performance)
Dear Student/Parent, in order to help us provide you with the highest quality instruction, please take a moment to complete this survey. You do not need to provide your name if you prefer.

Please tick the appropriate answer(s): Gender: Male ☐ Female ☐
Current Rank: _____
Age: under 12 ☐ over 12 ☐
Class Time and Days : _____

1. Your original goals for joining our school were to:
   Learn self defence ☐ Get in shape ☐ Improve self confidence ☐
   Relieve stress ☐ Improve self discipline ☐ Increase concentration ☐
   Other _____

2. Has the curriculum helped you meet your original goals?
   Yes ☐ No ☐
   Comments? _____

3. The curriculum being taught at my current rank seems to be:
   Too easy ☐ Just right ☐ Too difficult ☐
   Please explain _____

4. The quantity of material required at my current rank is:
   Not enough ☐ Just right ☐ Too much ☐
   Please explain if it needs adjusting. _____

5. Do you feel we cover your curriculum adequately before testing?
   Yes ☐ No ☐

6. How would you rate your instructor's presentation of the curriculum?
Poor ☐ Fair ☐ Good ☐ Great ☐
Comments: _____

7. Do you feel that you are taught realistic self-defence?
Yes ☐ No ☐
What would you like to see more of in the school? Example: more sparring, seminars, etc.

_____

What would you like to see less of in the school?

_____

8. For your lifestyle, what class length would work best for you?
30 minutes ☐ 45 minutes ☐ 1 hour ☐ 1.5 hours ☐

9. Given the value of your training, the customer service, extra classes, facilities and expertise we provide, how much do you feel our classes are worth monthly?
Less than £100 per month ☐ More than £100.00 per month ☐
Classes are priceless! ☐

10. What are you training goals now?
Black Belt. ☐ Fitness/Weight loss ☐ Become an instructor ☐
Become an Assistant Instructor ☐

Thank you very much for taking the time to complete the survey. How would you like to be notified about the actions we have taken as a result of this survey?

In person ☐ via email ☐ over the phone ☐ via text message ☐ in a letter ☐

Make sure to analyse the answers without delay to see if there are any immediate steps that need taking. If your students put their names on the survey it might be a good idea to give them some feedback on what you have done about any points they might have raised.

Resist the urge to respond to every single comment and/or suggestion you might get. Remember you can't please everybody. In fact, you might get contradicting views from students in the same class, some might state that the classes are too long whilst others would like them to be a bit longer. Instead, try to look for trends. If a dozen people tell you that the biggest class is over subscribed or that the Pro-Shop could do with more weapons, then you need to pick up on that feedback and make some changes.

RAPID RECAP – KEEPING STUDENTS HAPPY

- A certain level of attrition is normal in any martial arts school, but if you don't keep students happy you'll lose more than you should.
- Everybody leaves eventually, it's nothing personal. Make sure to have enough new students to replace those who have left.
- It is easier and cheaper to look after existing students than search and enrol new ones. Love your students and show that you care.
- Build good rapport with each student/parent by making them feel welcome and special.
- People don't like change. Resist the urge to chop and change things around too often or you will drive students away.
- Your reception is the nerve centre of your school. Look after it and train staff well to look after new and existing students.
- Complaints are vital feedback to help you improve things. Don't argue but listen carefully what people have to say to you before they tell everybody else. Thank them for their input and fix things fast.

SUMMARY

I sincerely hope that the information you found in this book will be of some use to you in starting and growing your own school. The contents of this book should give you a significant head start and edge over your competition. I wish I had access to this kind of information when I first started out.

You need to remember that success is not a matter of luck! OK, it certainly helps as when we get lucky, but luck really is just where preparation meets opportunity.

In business, like in any martial arts or combat system, it is always mind over matter. It is therefore important that you understand that there is a certain mind frame, which will enable you to approach a business venture, such as starting and running a martial arts school.

The key to becoming and staying successful is certainly good planning and consistency, but above all an unbridled love and passion for what you do. You need to realise that teaching martial arts classes is perhaps the least time consuming aspect of running a school. Create a supporting environment that will help you to overcome low points and challenges. The last thing you need is to deal with other people's envy and negativity.

Nothing will help you more to stay on course than clarity of what you are about, what your core business is as well as understanding what the key areas of your martial arts business are. This coupled with a clear vision of where you want your business to be in the next three to five years will set you up to meet many of the short term setbacks you might experience.

It will also enable you to allocate and prioritise your time, effort and resources so that none of these essential areas falls behind and therefore hamper you growth. Regardless of what type of business you want to run you are ultimately to blame for all decisions and shortcomings. The sooner you accept responsibility for all areas of your business the sooner you will be able to grow and succeed.

The more you try to be everything to everybody the more you are nothing to nobody. Realise and embrace your strengths and the opportunities that come with them and become known as the expert for your particular expertise. The more specific and clear you are about what you have to offer the better. Make sure that this is reflected in your branding and marketing.

Planning is as essential as breathing. This book gives you enough guidance to cover your basics but don't get bogged down in endless planning that leads to inaction. Much of what characterises successful entrepreneurs is their ability to deal with uncertainty and the things you cannot plan for.

Remember that everybody leaves in the end. It is your responsibility to draw out this point of departure through outstanding customer service by always under-promising and always over-delivering. This needs to go hand-in-hand with a constant recruitment drive to ensure that you don't get caught out by unexpected events. Try to have as many marketing tools as possible working for you to get a consistent yield of leads. The best and most cost effective way by far, is to grow through referrals. Use Social Media wisely to that effect.

Teaching, just like business, needs proper planning and preparation. Ensure that you have clearly defined learning outcomes for your students to remove any guess work. Frequent chopping and changing will confuse and alienate your students and erode you student base.

Become a friend of numbers as you can only control what you can measure. Resist the temptation to pass this on to others too soon, as you could end up flying blind, with little or no warning to respond to potential threads.

Above all have fun and embrace this massive learning curve. Your unbridled passion to seeing your students succeed is what will get you there.

THE DREAM KILLER

I saved the worst mistake in running a successful martial arts school for last. Not only is it the biggest mistake, it is by far the most common mistake of them all.

Forewarned is forearmed, as they say and I know that the prospect of doing it alone can be daunting. Even if you mange to follow all the advice and avoid all the mistakes I mentioned here, you still might not be a success. However, I believe that the worst thing you can do is not to at least try it out.

Working for yourself, creating a thriving martial arts business that inspires and nurtures its students, is truly one of the most remarkable journeys you can embark upon. I have spoken to many instructors over the years and many have come up with excuses for why they haven't set-up their own school yet; they didn't have time or the money or the skills or the experience or even the courage to do so. Which one of those will stop you fulfilling your dream of your own full-time school? Just think where you want to be five years from now and how gutted you will be for not even attempting it and thinking of what could have been. You might be kicking yourself so hard; the bruise would probably never go away.

RECOMMENDED READING LIST

"The Seven Habits Of Highly Effective People", Stephen R. Covey

"The E-Myth Revisited", Michael E. Gerber

"Influence: The Psychology of Persuasion", Robert Cialdini

"Guerrilla Marketing", Jay Conrad Levinson

"Eat That Frog", Brian Tracey

"The One Minute Manager", Ken Blanchard

"Who Moved My Cheese", Spencer Johnson

"Natural Born Winners, Robin Sieger

"The Miracle Of Self-Discipline", Brian Tracy

"Excuses Be Gone! How to change lifelong, self-defeating thinking habits",Dr. Wayne W. Dyer

"The Psychology of Selling", Brian Tracy

"The 4-Hour Work Week", Timothy Ferris

ONLINE RESOURCES LIST

Please check out the KickStart website for up-to-date links.

This book's website:
www.martialartsbusinessschool.com

Geoff Thompson's website:
www.geoffthompson.com

The Charity Commission:
www.charitycommission.gov.uk.

Safer Activities For Everyone
(CRB checks and child protection training)
www.safechild.co.uk

The Disability Martial Arts Association
www.disabilitymartialartsassociation.co.uk

Online Printing
www.printcarrier.com or fairprint.co.uk.

Everything for five Dollars. From designs, reviews, SEO, etc.
www.fiverr.com

Leadboxes
leadbox.com or www.future-fitness.com

From car door magnets, business cards, letter headed paper to window decal stickers
www.vistaprint.co.uk

Mobile Card Payments

www.izettle.com

Royalty Free Images

www.istockphotos.com, www.gettyimages.co.uk or
www.martialartsgraphics.net

Club Retention Postcards and Loyalty Stickers

www.merit-badges.com

Newsletters and Auto-responders

www.constantcontact.com, www.mailchimp.com,
www.aweber.com

Free Online Surveys

www.surveymonkey.com

ABOUT THE AUTHOR

Talib Fehlhaber

Talib is a veteran of the martial arts with over thirty years of practical experience. He has been very successful in training and mentoring people since 1993. He has trained members of the U.S. Army to become self-defence instructors as well as conducting self-defence tutorials and sessions for the Chamber of Commerce, Norwich City College and the John Innes Institute.

Born in Germany in 1965, Talib was first introduced to the martial arts at the tender age of six, when his father tried to channel the lively boy and proceeded to enrol him at a local Judo club. This was the beginning of a lasting love affair with the fighting arts that has endured until today. He currently holds a fifth degree Black Belt level in Wing Chun Kung Fu. In 2007 he was recognised by the International Wing Tsun Masters Academy, Germany and officially awarded his Sifu title in recognition of his long standing engagement in teaching and promoting Wing Chun Kung Fu.

In a life time effort to keep his teaching practical and relevant he has devised his own method that he calls "Dynamic Wing Chun Kung Fu". As the name suggests it is broadly based on Wing Chun, but incorporates and integrates ideas of other fighting disciplines, especially when it comes to weapons. He is the founder and chief instructor of the Rapid Defence Martial Arts Academy in Norwich, which he set-up in 2004.

Dear Reader,

As mentioned in the introduction I am giving away a free online course included in the purchase price of this book. This should help you to get on with the most important aspect of learning, which is implementation.

Please go to the website for this book and register for free: www.martialartsbusinessschool.com/freecourse

Looking forward to seeing you on the other side.

To your success!
Talib Fehlhaber